Java

Practical Guide for Programmers

The Morgan Kaufmann Practical Guides Series
Series Editor: Michael J. Donahoo

Java: Practical Guide for Programmers
Zbigniew M. Sikora

Multicast Sockets: Practical Guide for Programmers
David Makofske and Kevin Almeroth

The Struts Framework: Practical Guide for Java Programmers
Sue Spielman

TCP/IP Sockets in Java: Practical Guide for Programmers
Kenneth L. Calvert and Michael J. Donahoo

TCP/IP Sockets in C: Practical Guide for Programmers
Michael J. Donahoo and Kenneth L. Calvert

JDBC: Practical Guide for Java Programmers
Gregory D. Speegle

For further information on these books and for a list of forthcoming titles,
please visit our Web site at *www.mkp.com/practical.*

Java

Practical Guide for Programmers

Zbigniew M. Sikora

Independent Consultant

MORGAN KAUFMANN PUBLISHERS

AN IMPRINT OF ELSEVIER SCIENCE

AMSTERDAM   BOSTON   LONDON   NEW YORK
OXFORD   PARIS   SAN DIEGO   SAN FRANCISCO
SINGAPORE   SYDNEY   TOKYO

Senior Editor   Rick Adams
Publishing Services Manager   Edward Wade
Developmental Editor   Karyn Johnson
Cover Design   Yvo Riezebos Design
Cover Image   Siede Preis/Getty Images
Text Design   Side by Side Studios/Mark Ong
Composition and Illustration   Windfall Software, using ZzTeX
Copyeditor   Robert Fiske
Proofreader   Sarah Burgundy
Indexer   Steve Rath
Interior Printer   The Maple-Vail Book Manufacturing Group
Cover Printer   Phoenix Color Corporation

Designations used by companies to distinguish their products are often claimed as trademarks or registered trademarks. In all instances in which Morgan Kaufmann Publishers is aware of a claim, the product names appear in initial capital or all capital letters. Readers, however, should contact the appropriate companies for more complete information regarding trademarks and registration.

Morgan Kaufmann Publishers
An Imprint of Elsevier Science
340 Pine Street, Sixth Floor
San Francisco, CA 94104-3205
www.mkp.com

07   06   05   04   03   5   4   3   2   1

Library of Congress Control Number: 2002114098
ISBN: 1-55860-909-1

This book is printed on acid-free paper.

To my mother, Janina

Contents

Preface

The purpose of this book is to help you quickly learn the essentials of the Java language. After its release in 1995, Java was initially used to execute programs from a Web page by means of applets. However, Java is also a general-purpose, object-oriented programming language. Java is used for developing applications as diverse as statistical calculations, graphics, and accessing databases in a multitiered environment. In contrast to other languages, Java has from the start supplied a large number of libraries. The latest release of Java 2 Standard Edition version 1.4, or J2SE 1.4, in February 2002 contains over 2000 classes. All this means that Java is huge, and possible applications of it are very diverse. Furthermore, many Java books tend to be huge, and though fine as reference material, do not serve the newcomer to Java desiring a concise introduction. This book focuses on the core language features only, and with the exception of Swing, does not cover any of the application libraries.

This book is aimed at students and professional programmers who have some knowledge of programming and are switching to Java. Experience of an objected-oriented or procedural language such as C++, Smalltalk, C, or Pascal is assumed. The book will be suitable for students in upper-division undergraduate or graduate Java conversion courses. It is not aimed at students learning to program. Professional programmers switching to Java will find a rapid introduction to the core language. This will give them the necessary Java background for tackling more specialist material such as J2EE. For example, students and enterprise programmers will find this book provides the Java needed for Gregory Speegle's JDBC book in this series. This book covers only basic features, and topics such as networking, RMI, and JavaBeans have not been included.

Recognizing that a programming language is best learned through example, we provide numerous program examples with line-by-line explanations. To maintain the book's conciseness and clarity, the program examples are not production-quality code. For example, exception handling is omitted from most of the examples, except, of course, in the chapter on exception handling. This concise, essentials-only approach is in line with the *Practical Guide* series over-all philosophy. The book is based on J2SE 1.4, but anyone using version 1.2 or 1.3 should have no difficulties since any 1.4 or 1.3 features have been explicitly highlighted in the text.

Chapter 1 dives straight in with a simple example of a Java program. This is to give you an early feel for the language and show where we are heading. Chapters 2 and 3 cover much of the basic syntax of Java, including sequencing, branching, and looping, but leaves discussion of object-oriented topics for later. Those of you with a background in C or C++ will be able to get quickly through these chapters. Chapters 4 and 5 cover the object-oriented features of the language. Chapters 6 and 7 cover the core features of exception handling and input/output. To this point, the chapters should be read in order. The last three chapters may be regarded as optional by some instructors. Chapter 8 covers the Swing graphical user interface, which is the one application area covered in the book. Developing GUIs is more fun, and readers coming from an environment such as C will appreciate what is included for free with Java. Chapter 9 discusses collections. Finally, Chapter 10 covers the more advanced topic of threads. This chapter uses applets for some of its examples, so you should familiarize yourselves with the applet material in Chapter 8 before attempting threads.

Source code, exercises, and related material can be found at the book's accompanying Web site, *www.mkp.com/practical/java.*

Acknowledgments

First I would like to thank the technical editor of the *Practical Guide* series, Dr. Jeff Donahoo of Baylor University, for his advice and numerous suggestions at all stages of the book's development. This is really appreciated. I would like to thank the reviewers. These include Carl Burnham; John Raley, Moonlight Systems; Lynn R. Ziegler, Saint John's University; An Lam, 3PARdata and U.C. Santa Cruz; Bill Jackson, Ensemble Studios; Dr. Lawrence (Pete) Petersen, Texas A&M University; Jonathan L. Brisbin; Christopher Marshall, JP Morgan; William Cox, Cox Consulting; Simon P. Chappell; Ryan Witcher, Modulant Solutions. All the reviewers provided considerable feedback and this has influenced the final version of the book. I would also like to thank the staff at Morgan Kaufmann, especially Karyn Johnson for her professionalism and, for giving me the opportunity to publish the book, Edward Wade, Cheri Palmer, and the rest of the production team.

chapter 1

Introduction

The Java language was released in 1995 at the time of explosive growth in the Internet. The initial language release included the HotJava Web browser written in Java itself. This made it possible for the browser to execute programs from a Web page by means of **applets**. Shortly after, Netscape and Microsoft enabled their browsers to execute Java applets.

However, Java is also a fully computational object-oriented language. As such, it is a suitable vehicle for conventional standalone programs or **applications**, which is the main use of the language today.

Java is also a multithreaded language, and this feature makes it a highly scaleable language for programs that execute on a Web server. Consequently, in recent years, there has been increasing use of Java for server side, or **servlet**, programming.

1.1 Simple Java Application

To give you an early feel for the language, the Multiply.java example shows a Java application that outputs the product of two integers supplied as parameters.

Multiply.java

```
1   public class Multiply {
2
3       public static void main(String[] args) {
4           String resultString;
5           int arg1;
6           int arg2;
7           int result;
8
9           arg1 = Integer.parseInt(args[0]);
10          arg2 = Integer.parseInt(args[1]);
11          result = arg1 * arg2;
```

```
12          resultString = Integer.toString(result);
13          System.out.println("The product of " + args[0] +
14          " and " + args[1] + " is " + resultString);
15     }
16  }
```

The program consists of a class, Multiply, in a source file, Multiply.java. We will cover classes in detail in Chapter 4. At this stage, it is sufficient to note that every program must contain one public class. public is an access modifier, which specifies that other programs can access our class. We discuss access modifiers in Chapter 5. We can determine the class from the declaration (line 1)

```
public class Multiply {
```

The source file name must be the same as the class name. The source file suffix must be .java. If these two conditions are not met, the program will not compile. The program is compiled using the javac compiler, for example,

```
> javac Multiply.java
```

where > is the command prompt. We use > to indicate a command prompt in general. This could be a > on Windows or a % on Unix. If compilation is successful, the compiler will produce a bytecode file Multiply.class. All compiled bytecode files have the suffix .class.

With many programming languages, compilation produces machine code. Each platform will have its own machine-specific code, so a program compiled on one platform will need to be recompiled on another before it can be run. Java bytecode is an intermediate code between source code and machine code. The bytecode can be run by any Java interpreter that conforms to the Java Virtual Machine (JVM) specification. A JVM can be a standalone interpreter or embedded in a browser or electronic device. So having produced our bytecode on one platform, we can run it on any other platform that supports a JVM.

To run the application, we can use the java interpreter as follows:

```
> java Multiply 7 12
The product of 7 and 12 is 84
```

Note that we do not add the .class suffix when specifying the program name. Following the program name are optional parameters separated by one or more spaces.

At this stage, we do not expect you to have a detailed understanding of the code. The starting brace, {, in line 1 denotes that following statements are part of the Multiply class. Line 16 consists of a closing brace, }, which denotes the end of the class. We use these braces not just to delimit classes but also, for example, to delimit blocks of code that follow an if or else statement.

Because the program is a standalone application, it must contain the declaration (line 3)

```
public static void main(String[] args) {
```

We will describe the keywords public, static, and void in later chapters. At this point, you should just note that they must precede main in the declaration line. A method is roughly equivalent to a procedure or function in a nonobject-oriented language. Every Java application must have a main method.

Note that Java is case sensitive; using PUBLIC instead of public, for example, will be rejected by the compiler.

The main method has as a parameter an array of String objects named args. The declarations (lines 4–7)

```
String resultString;
int arg1;
int arg2;
int result;
```

declare variables of type String and int. Note that a semicolon is used as a terminator, so statements can span more than one line.

The statement in line 9 takes the first supplied parameter, the first element in the args array identified by args[0], and converts it to the int type variable arg1. This is done using the parseInt method of the supplied Java language class Integer. The syntax for calling static methods, such as parseInt, is classname.methodname, or Integer.parseInt in our case. We will learn about static methods in Chapter 4. Line 11 multiplies the two input parameters, and line 12 converts the result to a String variable, resultString, using the supplied Integer.toString method.

In lines 13–14, System.out.println prints a line to the standard output stream, then terminates the line. System.out is an object in the java.lang.System class, which is of type java.io.PrintStream. In turn, println is a method within the PrintStream class, which takes a String as a parameter. This format of objectname.methodname(parameters) for invoking a method, which is not static, is standard Java syntax.

There are two main types of development environments in Java. The first is the Software Development Kit (SDK), which can be downloaded for free from Sun's Web site, *java.sun.com/j2se/1.4/download.html*. This site contains installation instructions for Windows, Solaris, and Linux environments, as well as a link to start the download itself. The SDK contains the javac compiler and java interpreter, various Java libraries, and tools. Once Java has been installed, programs are typically developed using a text editor and compiled and run from the command line as we have shown. Sun also provides a portal, *java.sun.com*, for Java in general. In particular, there is a link to the Java 2 Platform API (application programming interface) Specification. This provides documentation about all the Java-supplied classes and methods. The API documentation can be viewed online or downloaded.

The second kind of development environment is an IDE (integrated development environment) available from many sources such as Borland's JBuilder, Oracle's JDeveloper, and Sun's Forte. Some of these are free for personal use in a nonproduction environment. These IDEs are window-driven environments and have all the SDK features as well as features such as default code generation, advanced debugging, and code coaches. Compiling or running a Java program can be done by clicking on a menu or tool bar in the IDE. A typical development feature is to bring up a list of methods in a popup window once a class or object has been typed, thereby doing away with the need to memorize the large number of methods provided by the Java libraries. Although IDEs are fine tools for experienced Java developers, they have a large number of features that have to be assimilated. If you are new to both Java and IDEs, you will find yourself at first spending as much time learning about the IDE as Java itself.

In the remainder of this book, we will use the convention of

```
> javac MyClass.java
> java MyClass
```

to indicate compiling or running Java programs, whether from the command line SDK or a Windows-driven IDE. To distinguish user input from any output, we will use the convention of highlighting user input in bold.

1.2   Java Tools

The Java SDK contains a number of tools that are executed from the command line. If an IDE is being used, then many of these tools will be incorporated within the IDE. We have already encountered javac and java; we will describe these in a little more detail here. Other tools such as javadoc and jar will be covered later in the book.

1.2.1   javac

javac compiles Java source code and produces bytecode class files. The source code file must have a .java suffix; the resulting class files have a .class suffix. The file must contain one public class with the class name the same as the file name. Other nonpublic classes can be included in the same file. We can include more than one source file in a single command, for example

```
javac Class1.java Class2.java
```

We can also group several source files in a single command file. For example, Myfiles could contain

```
Class1.java
Class2.java
Class3.java
```

These can all be compiled with the command

```
javac @Myfiles
```

A program will usually have references to other classes. javac will search for a corresponding class file. If a class file is found, but no corresponding source file, javac will use the class file. If a corresponding source file is found, but no class file, javac will compile the source file and use the resulting class file. If both source file and class file are found, the class file is used unless the source file is more recent than the class file, in which case the source file is recompiled and the resulting class file is used.

javac has a number of associated options: we will cover just a few.

```
-d destination
```

This sets the destination directory for the resulting class file. The default is to place the class file in the same directory as the source file.

```
-verbose
```

This outputs details about each class loaded and each source file compiled.

javac, as well as java, also have a classpath option. We will discuss this option in Chapter 5 after we have covered packages.

1.2.2 java

The java interpreter runs Java applications. It loads the application's class file and invokes the specified class's main method, which must be public, void, and static. There are a number of options for java, including the verbose option that we have seen for the javac compiler. The format of the command is

```
java [options] classname  [program parameters]
```

Note you do not include the .class suffix in the class name.

1.3 **Language Features**

Java's portability is largely achieved through the Java Virtual Machine concept. Instead of compiling a program to a machine-specific code, a Java program is compiled into a machine-independent bytecode. The bytecode, in turn, is interpreted by a machine-specific Java Virtual Machine (JVM). A JVM is small, so it can easily be incorporated into Web browsers. JVMs are available in many other environments: a standalone JVM can be downloaded from Sun's Web site; JVMs can be included in personal digital assistants (PDAs), or incorporated into relational database engines such as Oracle, or integrated development environments (IDEs) such as Borland's JBuilder.

This approach means that Java program execution will be slower than a C program, for example. Java, however, is significantly faster than other interpreted languages such as Smalltalk. There can be further performance improvements with the use of just-in-time (JIT) compilers that compile the bytecode into machine-specific code on demand.

Portability is also achieved by having a machine-independent size for all primitive data types such as integer and floating point numbers. This contrasts with C, where maximum sizes are machine dependent.

This has led to Sun describing Java as "write once, run everywhere." However, this claim is compromised to an extent. For example, the latest versions of most Web browsers support only Java version 1.1. Java version 1.2 applets, which may include features such as Swing, cannot be executed by most browsers. You can get around this by installing a Java 1.2 plugin to run with the browser, but this does qualify the "write once, run everywhere" claim.

Java is an object-oriented language. Object-oriented programming encourages good software engineering practices such as information hiding and code reuse. Object technology has a long history. The first fully object-oriented language, Smalltalk, was developed in 1972 although object features were present in the Simula language before then. The most widely used object-oriented language prior to Java was C++. This was developed in 1985 by adding object features to the then widely used C language.

In contrast to C and C++, explicit memory allocation and deallocation is not required in Java. The Java runtime system uses automatic garbage collection to reclaim memory of objects no longer in use. There is no explicit use of pointers in Java programs. Pointers can corrupt areas of memory, producing side effects and consequently making debugging a difficult process. Pointers can even cause the underlying operating system to crash. However, Java shares much of the syntax for data types and control structures with C.

Java differs from pure object languages such as Smalltalk in that primitive data types are not treated as objects in Java for efficiency purposes. Java does provide object wrapper classes for primitive data types for situations where their use is required. Java, through the bytecode compilation process, is faster than the purely interpreted Smalltalk language.

Java is a multithreaded language. Threads are concurrent executions of code under control of a single parent program. Threads can be explicitly created by application programs. Multithreading leads to improved performance and scalability. Java is also a dynamic language: classes are loaded only as they are needed.

Java provides a rich set of classes, or application programming interfaces (APIs). Some of these classes such as input/output or the windowing classes of the Abstract Windows Toolkit (AWT) are part of the language, and therefore are included with Java language releases. Other APIs, such as the Swing graphical user interface, Java Database Connectivity (JDBC), and servlets are considered separate from the language, and so can be released independently if required.

Basic Language Syntax

This chapter starts looking at the basic syntax or grammar of the Java language. We use an example program to illustrate language basics such as variables, Java keywords, data types, and arithmetic operations. We suspend discussion of objects until Chapter 4 although we do cover strings and arrays in this chapter. We continue with the basic syntax in Chapter 3, where we discuss topics related to program flow control.

Throughout this chapter, we use an example application, Circle, which calculates the area of a circle. The radius is input as a parameter to the program.

Circle

```
 1  /*
 2  This application reads in a radius of a circle
 3  and outputs its area.
 4  */
 5
 6  public class Circle {
 7      static final double PI = 3.14159;
 8
 9      public static void main(String[] args) {
10          int radius;
11          double area;
12
13          radius = Integer.parseInt(args[0]);
14          // area formula
15          area = PI * (radius * radius);
16          System.out.println("A circle of radius  " + args[0]
```

```
17              + " has area of " + area);
18      }
19  }
```

Circle

An example of the output of `Circle` is as follows:

```
> java Circle 5
A circle of radius 5 has area of 78.53975
```

2.1 Comments

Comments are included in a program's code to improve readability, and are ignored by the Java compiler. Comments that span one or more lines are enclosed by /* and */. In the `Circle` program, lines 1–4 is an example of a multiline comment.

A single line comment is prefixed by //. A single line comment may be appended to an existing statement. An example of a single line comment in line 14 is

```
// area formula.
```

2.1.1 javadoc

The `javadoc` tool, available as part of the Java SDK, parses documentation comments within a Java source file and produces an HTML document. Within the source file, such comments are included in a block beginning with /** and ending with */. Comment text is written in HTML format and will include tags, prefixed with a @, which can be used, for example, for headings such as author name and program version number, and for creating hypertext links. Document blocks are placed immediately before the class, method, or field they describe.

`javadoc` can be used for documenting one or more classes, packages, or both packages and classes. We will learn about packages in Chapter 5. For each class or package, `javadoc` will produce an HTML file (of the form `class.html` or `package.html`), as well as a number of supporting files (`index.html`, for example). The resulting documentation has the same format as the Java 2 Platform API Specification.

2.2 Statements

A statement is the smallest executable unit in a program, and is terminated by a semicolon. For example, line 13 reads

```
radius = Integer.parseInt(args[0]);
```

One or more statements can be combined to form a block. A block is enclosed by braces { and }. All the code making up the `main` method, lines 9–18, is a block. Blocks can be nested to any depth; in our example, the `main` block is enclosed by the `Circle` class block.

2.3 Variables

A variable is used to store data in the computer's memory, which can later be used by the program. `radius` and `area` are examples of variables in the `Circle` class.

A declaration associates a variable with a type. For example, in line 10,

```
int radius;
```

declares an `int` type variable named `radius`. Any number of variables can be declared with a single data type so

```
int radius, diameter;
```

is a valid declaration. However, it is good practice to have one declaration per line. This makes it easier to add comments or to subsequently change a variable's data type. A variable can be assigned a value in the declaration. For example,

```
int radius = 5;
```

declares an integer variable `radius` and assigns it a value of 5. Of course, an alternative is to have separate declaration and assignment statements, as follows:

```
int radius;
...  other variable declarations
radius = 5;
```

A variable is an example of an **identifier**. An identifier is a named item that could be a variable, class, object, method—in fact, any Java construct. For example, `Circle` is a class identifier. An identifier can consist of an unlimited number of letters, digits, and underscores, but must start with a letter or underscore. A number of words are reserved by Java and cannot be used as identifiers; these are shown in Table 2.1.

As well as following the rules about identifiers, variables must also be unique within their scope. For example, within the scope of the `main` method of the `Circle` class, there can be only one variable named `radius`. A second declaration of `radius`, of type `float`, say, is illegal and would be rejected by the compiler.

2.4 Constants

In Java, we identify a constant by declaring it as `final`. Within the `main` method of the `Circle` class, we could have declared the PI constant as

```
final double PI = 3.14159;
```

Table 2.1: Java reserved words.

abstract	assert*	boolean	break	byte
case	catch	char	class	continue
default	do	double	else	extends
false	final	finally	float	for
goto**	if	implements	import	instanceof
int	interface	long	native	new
null	package	private	protected	public
return	short	static	strictfp	super
switch	synchronized	this	throw	throws
transient	true	try	void	volatile
while				

* assert has been introduced in J2SE 1.4.
** goto is a reserved word, but not part of the Java language.

However, PI can then be used only within the main method. If we were to add more methods to the Circle class, and want PI to be accessible to these methods, we need to declare PI within the Circle class block but outside the main method block, and prefix it with the static keyword. We have done this in line 7, as follows:

```
static final double PI = 3.14159;
```

A constant declared static is known as a **class constant**. We discuss the static concept further in Chapter 4. If PI were to be assigned a value subsequently in the program, this would be rejected by the compiler.

2.5   Data Types

We have already seen two data types, int and double. In this section, we describe all the data types available in Java. The integer and real number, boolean and character data types are all *primitive* data types. They are not objects mainly for efficiency purposes: this is in contrast to languages such as Smalltalk, where all data types are objects. Strings, arrays, and vectors, on the other hand, are objects in the Java language.

2.5.1   Integer Numbers

Integer variables or constants can take on only positive and negative integral values. Four integer types are available, as shown in Table 2.2.

All the integer types are stored internally as two's complement. A positive number is stored as its corresponding binary representation. For example, the byte representation of the number 3 will be 00000011. To store a negative number, all the bits of the corresponding

Table 2.2: Integer types.

Name	Size	Minimum Value	Maximum Value
byte	1 byte (8 bits)	−128	127
short	2 bytes (16 bits)	−32768	32767
int	4 bytes (32 bits)	−2147483648	2147483647
long	8 bytes (64 bits)	−9223372036854775808	9223372036854775807

positive binary number are inverted; then 1 is added to the result. For example, to obtain the byte representation of the number −4, we start with the binary representation of 4, 00000100. We invert the bits, resulting in 11111011. Finally, we add 1, resulting in 11111100. In this scheme, the sign is stored in the leftmost (high) bit: a zero indicating a positive number, and a one indicating a negative number.

Numbers larger than 1 byte are stored in **big-endian** order. The high-order (or most significant) byte is stored first in memory. **Little-endian** order follows the reverse convention. For example, take the short (2 byte) representation of the number 256: 00000001 00000000. The order conventions are

Address	Big-Endian Representation	Little-Endian Representation
00	00000001	00000000
01	00000000	00000001

int values are assigned as decimal values by default, as in

```
int i = 17;
```

To assign an octal value, prefix the value with a zero. For example,

```
int ioctal = 010;
```

assigns octal 10 (decimal 8) to ioctal.

To assign a hexadecimal value, prefix the value with a zero then an x. For example,

```
int ihex = 0xB;
```

assigns hexadecimal B (decimal 11) to ihex.

A long literal value has an l or L suffix, for example,

```
long lvar = 123456789L;
```

2.5.2 Real Numbers

For floating point, or real, numbers, two types are available, as shown in Table 2.3. Note that integer and real data types are guaranteed to take on the sizes in the preceding tables regardless of the hardware platform on which the program runs.

Table 2.3: Real types.

Name	Size	Minimum Value	Maximum Value
float	4 bytes (32 bits)	1.4E−45	3.4028235E38
double	8 bytes (64 bits)	4.9E−324	1.7976931348623157E308

When a literal value is assigned to a `float` variable, the value must be suffixed by an f or F, for example

```
float fvar = 6.2f;
```

The f indicates that 6.2 is a number of type `float`. By default, literal floating point numbers are of type `double`, but we can use a d or D suffix. So both the following are valid:

```
double dvar = 6.234;
double dvar = 6.234d;
```

2.5.3 Booleans

A **boolean** data type can take on only one of the literal values, **true** or **false**. For example,

```
boolean creditWorthy  = true;
if (creditWorthy) {
    System.out.println("Customer credit is good");
}
```

2.5.4 Characters

A character variable or constant is declared with the **char** keyword. A character takes on a single 16-bit Unicode character between single quotes. There are also a number of escape sequences for denoting special characters, as follows:

```
\t      tab
\r      carriage return
\n      line feed
\f      form feed
\b      backspace
\"      double quote
\'      single quote
\\      backslash
```

In the `Circle` program, we could add the following declaration immediately after the `PI` declaration in line 7:

```
static final char TAB = '\t';
```

The statement in lines 16–17 could be replaced by

```
System.out.println("A circle of radius  " + args[0]
                 + " has area of " + TAB  + area);
```

This will add a tab in the output string. We could have simply added \t in the output statement as in

```
System.out.println("A circle of radius  " + args[0]
                 + " has area of  \t " + area);
```

2.5.5   Strings

A string literal is made up of one or more characters between double quotes. An example of string literals is the statement in lines 16–17 of the Circle program. We can define a string to be a variable by using the **String** data type. For example, in the Circle program, we could declare String variables string1 and string2, as follows:

```
String string1 = "A circle of radius  ";
String string2 = " has area of " ;
```

Lines 16–17 can now be replaced by

```
System.out.println(string1 + args[0] + string2  + area);
```

The + is used as a concatenation operator. Where a `String` is concatenated with a value that is not a `String`, such as args[0] or area, the compiler will convert that value to a `String`.

A String is actually an object in Java; we discuss objects in detail in Chapter 4. A string can be created using the following objectlike syntax:

```
String string1 = new String("A circle of radius  ");
```

This statement, and the statement

```
String string1 = "A circle of radius  ";
```

are both legal in Java. An exception has been made in the Java language to allow initialization of a String in a manner similar to nonobject-oriented languages. An exception also has been made in the use of the + operator to allow String concatenation: we would expect to use a method to concatenate objects.

Since a `String` is an object, a large number of methods are provided for manipulating strings. For example, the java.lang.String.length method gives the length of a String, as in

```
string1.length()
```

The `java.lang.String.charAt(position)` method returns the character at the specified position, starting at 0. For example,

```
string1.charAt(3)
```

will return the fourth character in the string, namely, i.

Strings are **immutable** in Java. One cannot change individual characters in a `String`. There is no method to change the nth character in a `String`. When we perform `String` concatenation, we are not modifying the original `String` but creating a new `String` object. The following example of `java.lang.String.concat` method illustrates `String` immutability:

```
String s1, s2;
s1 = "abc";
s2 = s1.concat("def");
```

The value of s1 after the `concat` method is executed remains an unchanged "abc". s2 is equal to "abcdef" since `concat` returns a new object with the concatenated result, which is assigned to s2. The main advantage of `String` immutability is that the Java compiler can save space by sharing `Strings`. If a program repeatedly performs `String` concatenation, when processing a file, for example, then the repeated creation of new objects becomes inefficient. To cater for this, Java provides a **mutable** `StringBuffer` class, which we discuss in Chapter 4.

We can convert all primitive data types to a `String` using the `java.lang.String.valueOf` method. For example, the following converts an `int` to a `String`:

```
int count = 123;
String countString = String.valueOf(count);
```

2.5.6 Arrays

An **array** contains a collection of elements, all of which have the same type. Arrays can be of any type. An array declaration is of the form

```
datatype  variable_name [] ;
```

or

```
datatype [] variable_name;
```

We have already seen an array, args, of type `String` in the `Circle` program. If we wish to declare an array, intArray, say, of type int, enter either

```
int [] intArray;
```

or

```
int intArray[];
```

This statement only declares the variable intArray. To create or define an array, that is, reserve storage in memory to hold the array, we need to use the **new** keyword. For example,

```
intArray = new int [2];
```

will create the array intArray with two elements and initialize it with zero values, the default value for numbers. The reason for the new keyword is that an array is actually an object in Java. Objects in Java are created using the new keyword, as we shall see in Chapter 4.

Array elements are counted from zero, so

```
intArray[0] = 1;
```

assigns the value of 1 to the first element of intArray. Note that once an array is created, its size cannot be changed.

An example of all this is the OutputArray program, which assigns the values of 1 and 2 to an integer array and outputs the results.

OutputArray

```
 1  public class OutputArray {
 2
 3      public static void main(String[] args) {
 4          int intArray [];
 5          intArray = new int [2];
 6          intArray[0] = 1;
 7          intArray[1] = 2;
 8          System.out.println("Values of intArray are "
 9          + intArray[0] + " and " + intArray[1]);
10      }
11  }
```

OutputArray

One can declare, create, and assign initial values to an array in a single statement, so we can replace lines 4–7 with the statement

```
int intArray[] = {1,2};
```

Arrays of arrays can be constructed in Java, by using consecutive pairs of brackets: [][]. OutputTable populates a two-dimensional array or table of type int.

OutputTable

```
 1  public class OutputTable {
 2
 3      public static void main(String[] args) {
 4          int table [] [] = {
 5                              {1, 2},
 6                              {3, 4, 5}
 7                          };
 8          System.out.println("Values of table are "
```

```
 9                + table[0][0] + " , " + table[0][1] + " , "
10                + table[1][0] + " , " + table[1][1] + " , "
11                + table[1][2]);
12        }
13  }
```

OutputTable

The main array, `table`, consists of two subarrays, `table[0]` and `table[1]`. Note the subarrays can be of different lengths. We could have defined the table array as

```
int table [] [] = new int [2] [3];
```

and populated the array element by element.

To find the length of an array, use

```
array_name.length
```

So in our `table` array example, `table.length` returns the value 2, and `table[1].length` returns the value 3.

The reason we can have arrays of arrays is that an array, like all objects, is a **reference type**. This means that the memory address is stored in an array variable. The value of the variable is a **reference to** a value or, indeed, to another array. So `table[1][2]` is a reference to the value 5, while `table[0]` is a reference to the array with elements `table[0][0]` and `table[0][1]`. Figure 2.1 shows how the two-dimensional `table` array is implemented.

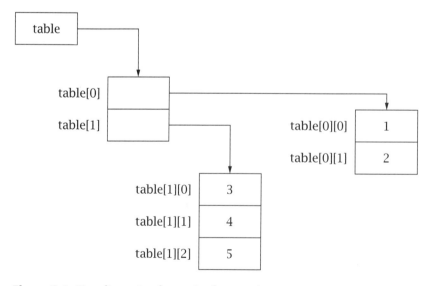

Figure 2.1: Two-dimensional array implementation.

2.6   Arithmetic Operations

The following arithmetic operators are available in Java:

+   addition
–   subtraction
*   multiplication
/   division
%   modulus

Java provides the ++ and – – operators, which, respectively, increment and decrement the operand. So a++ is equivalent to a = a + 1. If ++ or – – is postfixed to the operand, the result is evaluated before the increment or decrement. If ++ or – – is prefixed, the result is evaluated after the increment or decrement. The code in the Arithmetic example illustrates this.

Arithmetic

```
1   public class Arithmetic {
2
3       public static void main(String[] args) {
4           int a1 = 2;
5           int a2 = 2;
6           int a3 = 2;
7           int a4 = 2;
8           int b;
9           int c;
10          int d;
11          int e;
12
13          b = a1++;
14          c = ++a2;
15          d = a3--;
16          e = --a4;
17          System.out.println("a1 = " + a1 + " b = " +b );
18          System.out.println("a2 = " + a2 + " c = " +c );
19          System.out.println("a3 = " + a3 + " d = " +d );
20          System.out.println("a4 = " + a4 + " e = " +e );
21      }
22  }
```

Arithmetic

The output of the Arithmetic application is as follows:

```
> java Arithmetic
a1 = 3 b = 2
```

```
a2 = 3 c = 3
a3 = 1 d = 2
a4 = 1 e = 1
```

This idea is extended by the +=, -=, *=, /=, and %= operands to combine an operation with an assignment. Thus,

a += 2 is equivalent to a = a + 2

a -= 2 is equivalent to a = a - 2

a *= 2 is equivalent to a = a * 2

a /= 2 is equivalent to a = a / 2

a %= 2 is equivalent to a = a % 2

When an expression consists of two or more operators, Java applies rules of precedence about which operand is applied first. Operands with a higher precedence are applied before those of a lower precedence. The operands *, /, and % are of equal precedence, and are of higher precedence than + and -. Consequently,

8 * 4 - 2 is equivalent to (8 * 4) - 2, which equals 30

8 + 4 / 2 is equivalent to 8 + (4 / 2), which equals 10

Of course, you can use parentheses to override this default behavior. Thus,

8 * (4 - 2) will evaluate to 16

(8 + 4) / 2 will evaluate to 6

Where an expression consists of two or more operators of equal precedence, Java will in general evaluate the operands from left to right. For example,

8 / 4 * 2 is equivalent to (8 / 4) * 2, which equals 4

and not   8 / (4 * 2), which equals 1

The / and * operators are said to **associate** from left to right. A few operators associate from right to left. Appendix A lists all the operator associativity rules.

2.7 Data Type Conversion

We can assign one primitive data type to another provided there is no possible loss of precision. In such cases, Java automatically performs the data type conversion. For example, in the code fragment

```
short  s = 6;
int i = s;
```

we can assign s to i because the precision of a short is less than an int, so there is no possible loss of precision. However, the statement

```
s = i;
```

is illegal because there is possible loss of precision. The program will fail to compile. In this case, we need to explicitly **cast** the data type. This is done by enclosing the target data type with parentheses and prefixing this to the source variable. For example,

```
s = (short) i;
```

The loss of precision argument means that we can assign an int to a float, but we need to explicitly cast a float to an int, as follows:

```
float fvar = 6.2f;
int i = (int) fvar;
```

Note this truncates the fractional part. Even with a cast we cannot assign a boolean to an integer or real.

c h a p t e r **3**

Flow Control

$\mathbf{T}$his chapter concludes the basic language syntax with a discussion of sequencing, branching, and looping. We cover conditional statements, relational and logical operators, including bitwise operators, and iteration statements.

3.1 Conditional Statements

3.1.1 if Statement

The if construct is used if we wish to execute a statement only if a condition is true. The basic format of the if statement is

```
if (condition) {
   one or more statements to be executed if condition
   is true;
}
```

The following code fragment illustrates the if statement:

```
public static void main(String[] args) {
if (args.length == 1){
  System.out.println("Single argument = " + args[0] + " supplied");
}
System.out.println("no of args =  " + args.length);
}
```

Note there is no then component in the if clause in Java. The relational equality operator == is used in the statement

```
if (args.length == 1)
```

We will cover other relational operators in Section 3.2. If only one statement is executed when the condition is true, then the enclosing braces are optional. The preceding code could be rewritten as follows:

```
public static void main(String[] args) {
if (args.length == 1)
    System.out.println("Single argument = " + args[0] + " supplied");
System.out.println("no of args =  " + args.length);
}
```

However, it is good practice to always use braces even if a single statement follows the if condition. Otherwise, we might forget to add braces should a second embedded statement be subsequently added.

3.1.2   if else Statement

The if else construct is used if we wish to execute one set of statements if a condition is true, and a second set of statements if the condition is false. The basic format of the if else construct is as follows:

```
if (condition) {
    one or more statements to be executed if
    condition is true;
} else {
    one or more statements to be executed if
    condition is false;
}
```

To illustrate this, the CalculateProduct example calculates the square of an input argument if just one argument is supplied to the program; otherwise, it calculates the product of the first and second arguments.

CalculateProduct

```
1   public class CalculateProduct {
2
3       public static void main(String[] args) {
4           int arg1;
5           int arg2;
6           int result;
7
8           if (args.length == 1){
9               arg1 = Integer.parseInt(args[0]);
10              result = arg1 * arg1;
11              System.out.println("Square of " + args[0] + " is "
12              + result);
13          } else {
14              arg1 = Integer.parseInt(args[0]);
```

```
15          arg2 = Integer.parseInt(args[1]);
16          result = arg1 * arg2;
17          System.out.println("Product of " + args[0] +
18          " and " + args[1] + " = " + result);
19        }
20        System.out.println("no of args =  " + args.length);
21    }
22  }
```

CalculateProduct

3.1.3 else if Statement

We can qualify the else clause in the previous section by adding a further condition to be satisfied for the subsequent statements to be executed. This is done by using an else if clause in place of the else clause. This has the following construct:

```
if (condition1) {
    one or more statements to be executed
    if condition1 is true;
} else if (condition2) {
    one or more statements to be executed
    if condition1 is false and condition2 is true;
}
```

Any number of else if clauses can be associated with the first if clause, and these may be optionally followed by an else clause. For example, we can modify CalculateProduct to handle three conditions: one argument supplied, two arguments supplied and zero, three or more arguments supplied. The result is shown in the second version of CalculateProduct.

CalculateProduct—second version

```
1  public class CalculateProduct {
2
3      public static void main(String[] args) {
4          int arg1;
5          int arg2;
6          int result;
7
8          if (args.length == 1){
9              arg1 = Integer.parseInt(args[0]);
10             result = arg1 * arg1;
11             System.out.println("Square of " + args[0] + " is "
12             + result);
13         } else if (args.length == 2){
14             arg1 = Integer.parseInt(args[0]);
```

```
15              arg2 = Integer.parseInt(args[1]);
16              result = arg1 * arg2;
17              System.out.println("Product of " + args[0]
18              + " and " + args[1] + " = " + result);
19          } else {
20              System.out.println(
21              "Please supply one or two arguments");
22          }
23          System.out.println("no of args =  " + args.length);
24      }
25  }
```

CalculateProduct—second version

3.1.4   Embedded Conditional Expressions

The ? operator enables you to embed expressions that are conditional on the value of a boolean expression. The format is

```
boolean expression ? expression1 : expression2
```

expression1 is executed if the boolean expression is true; expression2 is executed if boolean expression is false. The following code uses the ? operator:

```
public static void main(String[] args) {
 System.out.println(args.length +
 (args.length == 1 ? " argument has been provided" :
  " arguments have been provided") );
}
```

The preceding code could be rewritten replacing the ? with the if else construct, as follows:

```
public static void main(String[] args) {
 if (args.length == 1){
   System.out.println(args.length + " argument has been provided");
 } else {
   System.out.println(args.length + " arguments have been provided");
 }
}
```

3.1.5   Switch Statement

Another type of branching construct is the switch statement. This takes the form

```
switch (expression1) {
case value1:
    one or more statements to be executed;
    break;
case value2:
```

```
            one or more statements to be executed;
            break;
      default:
            one or more statements to be executed;
            break;
      }
```

expression1 is a char, byte, short, or int expression evaluated by the switch statement. If this is equal to value1, the statements following the case value1: clause are executed. If expression1 evaluates to value2, the statements following case value2: are executed. Of course, there can be any number of case statements. If the value of expression1 is not included in any of the case statements, then the statements following default: are executed.

The break statement ensures that program execution continues with the statement following the entire switch block. Without a break statement, after executing the corresponding case statement, control would pass to subsequent case statements. As an example, the second version of CalculateProduct has been rewritten using the switch statement: the result is shown in the third version of CalculateProduct.

CalculateProduct—third version

```
 1  public class CalculateProduct {
 2
 3      public static void main(String[] args) {
 4          int arg1;
 5          int arg2;
 6          int result;
 7
 8          switch (args.length) {
 9          case 1:
10              arg1 = Integer.parseInt(args[0]);
11              result = arg1 * arg1;
12              System.out.println("Square of " + args[0] + " is "
13              + result);
14              break;
15          case 2:
16              arg1 = Integer.parseInt(args[0]);
17              arg2 = Integer.parseInt(args[1]);
18              result = arg1 * arg2;
19              System.out.println("Product of " + args[0] + " and "
20              + args[1] + " = " + result);
21              break;
22          default:
23              System.out.println(
24              "Please supply one or two arguments");
25              break;
26          }
```

```
27          System.out.println("no of args =  " + args.length);
28      }
29  }
```

CalculateProduct—third version

3.2   Relational and Logical Operators

We have already encountered the equals relational operator ==. Listed next are all the relational operators.

>   greater than
>=   greater than or equal to
<   less than
<=   less than or equal to

These are all of equal precedence. The remaining two operators are of lower precedence.

==   equals
!=   not equals

The precedence rules mean that in the following code fragment:

```
int  a = 5, b = 4;
boolean c = true;
if (a > b == c) {
    System.out.println("Condition true");
}
```

the condition a > b == c is equivalent to (a > b) == c. The expression a > b is evaluated first and returns a value of true or false, which is then compared with the value of the boolean variable c.

More complex condition expressions can be constructed with the use of logical operators, listed in order of precedence in Table 3.1.

Expressions using logical operators are evaluated left to right. Logical operators, apart from !, have a lower precedence than the relational operators. A complete list of precedence rules is shown in Appendix A.

The && and || operators have the same function as & and |, respectively, except in the manner in which component expressions are evaluated. For example, in the expression (a > b) & (c < d), the components are evaluated left to right, so (a > b) is evaluated first. If (a > b) is false, the entire expression is false regardless of the result of the component (c < d). Nevertheless, the component (c < d) will still be evaluated. However, in the expression (a > b) && (c < d), the component (c < d) will *not* be evaluated if (a > b) evaluates to false. This is known as **short circuiting**.

Table 3.1: Logical operators.

Operator	Meaning	Evaluation
!	not	n/a
&	and	unconditional
^	exclusive or (a or b true but not both)	unconditional
|	or (a or b true)	unconditional
&&	and	conditional
||	or (a or b true)	conditional

The following code fragment illustrates the use of logical operators:

```java
int a = 5, b = 4, c = 2, d = 3, e = 0;
if (! (a < b) ) {
    System.out.println(" ! condition true");
}
if ( (a > b) & (c < d) ) {
    System.out.println(" & condition true");
}
if ( (a > b) | (c < d) ) {
    System.out.println(" | condition true");
}
if ( (a > b) ^ (c < d) ) {
    System.out.println(" First ^ condition true");
} else {
    System.out.println(" First ^ condition false");
}
if ( (a > b) ^ (d < c) ) {
    System.out.println(" Second ^ condition true");
}
if ((true) | | (5/e == 0)) {
    System.out.println(" Divide by 0 avoided");
}
if ((true) | (5/e == 0)) {
    System.out.println(" Not printed");
}
```

This will output

```
> java TestLogicals
! condition true
& condition true
| condition true
First ^ condition false
Second ^ condition true
```

Table 3.2: Bitwise binary operations.

Operation	Result
a	00000011
b	00000010
a & b	00000010
a | b	00000011
a ∧ b	00000001

```
Divide by 0 avoided
java.lang.ArithmeticException: / by zero
    void TestLogicals.main(java.lang.String[])
Exception in thread main
```

Note that the first ∧ condition is false since both (a > b) and (c < d) are true.

3.2.1   Bitwise Operators

The bitwise operators, & (bitwise and), | (bitwise or), ∧ (bitwise exclusive or), and ~ (bitwise complement) are used to manipulate the bits of the Java integral types. The operators act similarly to the equivalent logical operators, except that operations apply to individual bits.

The & operator sets the resulting bit to 1 if the corresponding bit in both operands is 1; otherwise, the resulting bit is 0. The | operator sets the resulting bit to 1 if either bit is 1; otherwise, the resulting bit is 0. The ∧ operator sets the resulting bit to 1 if the two bits are different; otherwise, the resulting bit is 0. Table 3.2 shows the results of these bitwise binary operations applied to operands a and b, where a is the byte representation of the number 3, and b is the byte representation of the number 2.

The ~ (bitwise complement) operator is a unary operator that inverts the value of each bit of the operand.

Java also provides bit-shifting operators that apply to integral types. >> is a signed right shift, << a left shift, and >>> an unsigned right shift with the resulting top bits filled by the sign bit. The operators have a second right-hand operand that specifies the number of bits to shift. So, for example, i << 2 shifts the bits of int i by two to the left.

3.3   Iteration Statements

If we wish to repeatedly execute a block of statements while a condition is true, the while, do while, and for loop constructs are available.

3.3.1   while Loop

The syntax of a while loop is

```
while (boolean expression) {
  one or more statements;
}
```

The block of statements is repeatedly executed while the boolean expression evaluates to true. As an example, we can rewrite the OutputArray program of Section 2.5.6 and assign values to array elements intArray[0] and intArray[1] using a while loop.

OutputArray

```
1  public class OutputArray {
2
3      public static void main(String[] args) {
4          int i=0;
5          int intArray [];
6
7          intArray = new int [2];
8          while (i < intArray.length) {
9              intArray[i] = i + 1;
10             i++;
11         }
12         System.out.println("Values of intArray are " +
13         intArray[0] + " and " + intArray[1]);
14     }
15 }
```

OutputArray

3.3.2   do while Loop

The syntax of a do while loop is

```
do {
    one or more statements;
} while (boolean expression) ;
```

Unlike a while loop, a do while loop is guaranteed to execute at least once. In the OutputArray example of the previous section, the while loop (lines 8-11) can be replaced by the following do while loop:

```
do {
    intArray[i] = i + 1;
    i++;
} while (i < intArray.length);
```

3.3.3   for Loop

Where the iteration is over a range of values, a for loop is a more compact alternative to a while or do while loop. The syntax is

```
for (initialization expression;
        test expression;
        increment expression) {
            one or more statements;
}
```

The initialization expression is executed once at the beginning of the first loop iteration. The increment expression is executed at the end of every loop iteration. The test expression is evaluated at the beginning of each loop iteration. If the test expression evaluates to false, the for loop is terminated; if it evaluates to true, another iteration of the loop is executed. Like a while loop, it is possible that the for loop may not be executed for a single iteration.

In the OutputArray example of section 3.3.1, the while loop (lines 8–11) can be replaced by the following for loop:

```
for (i = 0; i < intArray.length; i++) {
    intArray[i] = i+1;
}
```

Note that initialization, i = 0; increment, i++; and test expression, i < intArray.length all occur on a single line. Any of the three parts of a for loop can be omitted, but the semicolons must remain. If all three parts are omitted, we have an infinite for loop, as follows:

```
for (;;) {
    ...
}
```

Within the for loop, there will be some means, such as a break statement, to end the looping.

3.3.4   break and continue Statements

We have already seen the break statement in the context of the switch statement. The break statement can also be used to exit out of a for, while, or do while loop. The SumOddArguments program sums all the arguments until the first even-valued argument is reached.

SumOddArguments

```
1  public class SumOddArguments {
2
3      public static void main(String[] args) {
4          int arg;
5          int sum = 0;
6
```

```
 7          for (int i = 0; i < args.length; i++) {
 8              arg = Integer.parseInt(args[i]);
 9              if (arg % 2 == 0) {
10                  break;
11              }
12              sum = sum + arg;
13          }
14          System.out.println("Sum of odd arguments is : " + sum);
15      }
16  }
```

SumOddArguments

In the for loop (lines 7–13), as soon as an even-valued argument has been reached, in line 9 arg % 2 is equal to 0; consequently, the break statement passes control to the first statement after the for loop, namely, line 14.

The continue statement passes control to the next iteration of the enclosing for, while, or do while loop. The following code fragment sums all odd integers from 1 to 10:

```
int sum = 0;
for (int i = 1; i < 11; i++) {
    if (i % 2 == 0) {
        continue;
    }
    sum = sum + i;
}
```

The continue statement ensures that, for an even number, the next statement, sum = sum + i, is skipped and thus sum is not incremented.

If within nested loops, a break statement is used to exit out of one of the inner loops, then control passes to the next iteration of the enclosing loop. If the intention is to break out of two or more enclosing loops, then this can be achieved by a labeled break. The SumSomeArguments example sums all arguments until one argument is equal to one of the elements of the array intArray. The elements of intArray are set to 5 and 6. If arguments of 7, 8, 9, 5, and 3, say, are passed to the program, then the resulting sum equals 7 + 8 + 9 = 24.

SumSomeArguments

```
1  public class SumSomeArguments {
2
3      public static void main(String[] args) {
4          int intArray [];
5          int arg;
6          int sum = 0;
```

```
7
8           intArray = new int [2];
9           intArray[0] = 5;
10          intArray[1] = 6;
11          outerForLoop:
12          for (int i = 0; i < args.length; i++) {
13              arg = Integer.parseInt(args[i]);
14              for (int j = 0; j < 2; j++) {
15                  if (intArray[j] == arg) {
16                      break outerForLoop;
17                  }
18              }
19              sum = sum + arg;
20          }
21          System.out.println("Sum of arguments =  " + sum);
22      }
23  }
```

SumSomeArguments

The label in line 11 is outerForLoop:. The syntax for a label is any valid identifier followed by a colon. The break label statement, break outerForLoop:, in line 16, will pass control to the statement following the statement identified by the label. The outerForLoop: statement refers to the entire outer for loop enclosed by braces, so control passes to the println statement in line 21. If we had used an unlabeled break in the program, then control would have passed to line 19, and the program would have carried on adding the arguments to the sum.

Classes and Objects

Two fundamental concepts in object-oriented programming are that of classes and objects. A *class* can be regarded as an object template: it describes how an object looks and operates. We may have a bank account class that holds details such as account number, account name, and balance. These are defined by **member variables** that are said to define the **state** of the class. Examples of operations associated with the bank account class are making a deposit or a withdrawal. *Operations,* or **methods** in object-oriented terminology, are said to define the **behavior** of a class. An *object* is an **instance** of a class. Corresponding to our bank account class, each individual bank account would be an object: fredsAccount, say, would be an object holding bank account details for the individual Fred. The following sections illustrate all the preceding concepts with Java code.

4.1 Class and Object with No Methods

To start, we will define a class, Account, corresponding to a bank account. This class will have member variables defined for account number, account name, and balance. At this stage, we have defined no methods for this class.

Account

```
1  class Account {
2      int accountNo;
3      String accountName;
4      double balance;
5  }
```

The class identifier, `Account`, in line 1 can be any valid Java identifier. By convention, class identifiers are nouns, in mixed case with the first letter of each internal word capitalized. Member variables are declared using the syntax datatype variableName as described in Section 2.3. The code must be stored in a file `Account.java`. Compilation by means of the command

>   `javac Account.java`

will create a compiled bytecode file `Account.class`.

We create, or instantiate, an object using the following syntax:

`classIdentifier objectName = new classIdentifier();`

So to create an object `fredsAccount` that is an instantiation of the `Account` class, we would use the following statement:

`Account fredsAccount = new Account();`

in any program, either an application or an applet, that uses the object.

To set the member variables to a particular value, we would use the syntax

`objectIdentifier.variableIdentifier = value;`

So to set the account number for `fredsAccount` object to a value of 123, say, we would use the statement

`fredsAccount.accountNo = 123;`

Bringing all this together is an application, `CreateAccount`, that creates the `fredsAccount` object, sets all the corresponding class member variables, and prints their values.

CreateAccount

```
 1  class CreateAccount {
 2
 3      public static void main(String[] args) {
 4          Account fredsAccount = new Account();
 5          fredsAccount.accountNo = 123;
 6          fredsAccount.accountName = "Fred";
 7          fredsAccount.balance = 50;
 8          System.out.println("A/c no: " + fredsAccount.accountNo +
 9          " A/c name: " + fredsAccount.accountName  + " Balance: "
10          +  fredsAccount.balance);
11      }
12  }
```

CreateAccount

We will need to compile CreateAccount by means of the command

```
> javac CreateAccount.java
```

Then we can run the program

```
> java CreateAccount
A/c no: 123 A/c name: Fred Balance: 50.0
```

4.2 Class with Methods

As we have already mentioned, as well as member variables defining its state, a class can have methods defining its behavior. A method is similar to a procedure or function in a nonobject-oriented programming language. For our bank account class, examples of methods are deposit and withdraw. The following is code for the deposit method that increases the balance by the amount deposited:

```
public void deposit(double amount) {
    balance = balance + amount;
}
```

The method declaration is of the form

```
access_modifier return_type identifier (arg1_type arg1_name, ...)
```

The access modifier for the deposit method example is public. This means that any class can access the deposit method. We will look at access modifiers in Chapter 5. The method return type can be any Java data type. If the method does not return a value, use the keyword void as though void were a data type. Since our deposit method does not return a value, we use void. The method identifier itself can be any valid Java identifier. Optionally, a method can have any number of arguments preceded by their data types. In the deposit method, we have one argument, amount, which is of type double. A method may have no arguments, in which case add () after the method identifier. For example,

```
public void clearBalance() {
    balance = 0;
}
```

The method body is enclosed in braces, { and }, and can have any number of statements. In the deposit method, we have just one statement

```
balance = balance + amount;
```

balance is an Account class member variable, so still is in scope in the deposit method. amount is a variable local to the deposit method, so cannot be accessed outside the deposit method.

In the case of a withdrawal from our bank account, the balance will be decreased by the amount withdrawn. If the resulting balance is less than zero, an error message is printed and no withdrawal is made. We would also like our method to return the value of the outstanding balance. The Java code for the withdraw method follows:

```java
public double withdraw(double amount) {
    if (balance - amount < 0) {
        System.out.println("Insufficient Funds");
    }
    else {
        balance = balance - amount;
    }
    return balance;
}
```

Later in Chapter 6, we will see how the Java exception mechanism provides a better way to report this condition.

Note the return statement in the withdraw method. A return statement is used to exit from a method. Control passes to the statement following the one that invoked the method. If a method is void, use the statement

```java
return;
```

to exit from the method. Note that control passes to the invoking method after the last statement in the current method, so a return statement is required in a void method only if we wish to prematurely exit from the method if some condition is met. For methods other than void, we need to use the statement

```java
return expression;
```

where expression is the same data type as the current method's return type. For non-void methods, the last statement in the method must be a return statement.

Note that since the withdraw method returns the balance, which is an Account class member variable of type double, the withdraw method is of type double. The Account class in this section now includes the deposit and withdraw methods.

Account

```java
1  class Account {
2      int accountNo;
3      String accountName;
4      double balance;
5  
6      public void deposit(double amount) {
7          balance = balance + amount;
8      }
9  
10     public double withdraw(double amount) {
11         if (balance - amount < 0) {
12             System.out.println("Insufficient Funds");
```

```
13          } else {
14              balance = balance - amount;
15          }
16          return balance;
17      }
18  }
```

The syntax for invoking a method is

```
object_identifier.method(optional arguments);
```

An example of statements invoking the deposit and withdraw methods of the Account class is

```
fredsAccount.deposit(100);
amountLeft = fredsAccount.withdraw(120);
```

where amountLeft is a variable of type double.

4.3 **Constructors**

Java provides a special kind of method, called a **constructor**, that executes each time an instance of an object is created. The constructor can be used to initialize the state of an object. The call to new, which creates an object, invokes the new object's constructor. The constructor has the same identifier as its class and does not define a return type. The following code fragment shows the Account constructor that sets the account number, name, and balance to supplied values:

```
public Account(int no, String name, double bal){
    accountNo = no;
    accountName = name;
    balance = bal;
}
```

This code would be added to the Account class definition in the same way as the deposit and withdrawal methods. The Account class now includes its constructor.

Account

```
1  class Account {
2      int accountNo;
3      String accountName;
4      double balance;
5
6      public Account(int no, String name, double bal) {
```

```
 7              accountNo = no;
 8              accountName = name;
 9              balance = bal;
10        }
11
12        public void deposit(double amount) {
13              balance = balance + amount;
14        }
15
16        public double withdraw(double amount) {
17              if (balance - amount < 0) {
18                    System.out.println("Insufficient Funds");
19              } else {
20                    balance = balance - amount;
21              }
22              return balance;
23        }
24 }
```

Account

The statements (lines 4-7) in the CreateAccount application in Section 4.1, which create the fredsAccount object and initialize the corresponding class member variables, can now be replaced by the single statement

```
Account fredsAccount = new Account(123, "Fred", 50);
```

If a class does not have a constructor, then Java creates a default constructor. This has no parameters, and all instance variables are set to their default values. So for the Account class, the default constructor will be equivalent to

```
public Account() {
    accountNo = 0;
    accountName = null;
    balance = 0.0;
    }
```

Consequently, the statement

```
Account fredsAccount = new Account();
```

is legal if the Account class does not have a constructor. However, if a class has one or more constructors and does not explicitly include a constructor without parameters, the preceding statement is illegal. We cannot rely on a default constructor as a fallback in this case.

4.4 Method Overloading

Method overloading is a feature common to most object-oriented programming languages and is one aspect of **polymorphism**. This allows us to have methods with the same identifier but with different argument lists. The argument lists can have a different ordering of data types or can have a different number of arguments. In the Account class, in addition to the deposit method we have already seen (lines 12–14), we could also add a second deposit method that prints the balance if it exceeds a supplied level.

```
public void deposit(double amount, double level) {
    balance = balance + amount;
    if (balance > level) {
        System.out.println("Current balance = " + balance);
    }
}
```

In the CreateAccounts application, the following statements would invoke each deposit method in turn:

```
fredsAccount.deposit(100);
fredsAccount.deposit(100, 120);
```

The Java compiler checks that the data types of the method being invoked match those of the method in the class. In this way, the correct method will be invoked.

Constructors can also be overloaded. In addition to the existing constructor in the Account class (lines 6–10), we can add a second, which takes only the account number and name as arguments and sets the balance to 10.

```
public Account(int no, String name) {
    accountNo = no;
    accountName = name;
    balance = 10;
}
```

In the CreateAccounts application, the following statements would create two objects, fredsAccount and billsAccount, using each constructor in turn:

```
Account fredsAccount = new Account(123, "Fred", 50);
Account billsAccount = new Account(456, "Bill");
```

4.5 Argument Passing in Java

Any valid Java data type can be passed as an argument into a method. These can be primitive data types such as int and float, or reference data types such as objects or arrays. Both primitive and reference data type arguments are passed by **value**; however, the impact on the calling method can be different depending on the passed data type.

Where a primitive data type argument is being passed, the **value** of the argument is copied into the method's parameter. If the method changes the value of the parameter, then this change is local to the method and does not affect the value of the argument in the calling program. The following example illustrates this. The Employee class consists of just one method, increment, which adds 10 to a supplied argument of type int.

Employee

```
1  class Employee {
2
3      public void increment(int amount) {
4          amount = amount + 10;
5          System.out.println("amount within method: " + amount);
6      }
7  }
```

Employee

The CreateEmployee application sets the variable amount to 500 and invokes the Employee class increment method with amount as an argument.

CreateEmployee

```
1  class CreateEmployee {
2
3      public static void main(String[] args) {
4          int amount = 500;
5
6          Employee fred = new Employee();
7          fred.increment(amount);
8          System.out.println("amount outside method: " + amount);
9      }
10 }
```

CreateEmployee

The output of running the CreateEmployee application follows:

```
> java CreateEmployee
amount within method: 510
amount outside method: 500
```

So although the increment method has increased the amount to 510, the amount in the calling program remains at 500.

If, however, the argument passed to a method is a reference data type, the memory **address** of the argument is copied to the method's parameter. Consequently, both the calling method argument and the called method parameter reference the same object. If the method changes the value of this object, then this change is reflected in the calling program. To illustrate this, the second version of Employee has the increment method modified to accept an array argument, salary, of type int. The first element of salary is incremented by 10.

Employee—second version

```
1  class Employee {
2
3      public void increment(int[] salary) {
4          salary[0] = salary[0] + 10;
5          System.out.println("amount within method: " +
6          salary[0]);
7      }
8  }
```

Employee—second version

In the second version of the CreateEmployee application, the argument passed to the increment method is an array, fredsSalary.

CreateEmployee—second version

```
1  class CreateEmployee {
2
3      public static void main(String[] args) {
4          int fredsSalary[] = new int [1];
5
6          Employee fred = new Employee();
7          fredsSalary[0] = 500;
8          fred.increment(fredsSalary);
9          System.out.println("amount outside method : "
10         + fredsSalary[0]);
11     }
12 }
```

CreateEmployee—second version

The output of running CreateEmployee will now be as follows:

```
> java CreateEmployee
amount within method: 510
amount outside method: 510
```

4.6 Instance and Static Variables

By default, class member variables are **instance** variables. In the Account class shown next, accountNo, accountName, and balance are all instance variables.

Account

```
1  class Account {
2      int accountNo;
3      String accountName;
4      double balance;
5  }
```

Account

Whenever an object, or instance, of the class is created, copies of the instance variables are created. In CreateAccount, two instances of the Account class are created: fredsAccount and billsAccount. The instance variables corresponding to fredsAccount and billsAccount are assigned values.

CreateAccount

```
1  class CreateAccount {
2
3      public static void main(String[] args) {
4          Account fredsAccount = new Account();
5          fredsAccount.accountNo = 123;
6          fredsAccount.accountName = "Fred";
7          fredsAccount.balance = 50;
8          Account billsAccount = new Account();
9          billsAccount.accountNo = 456;
10         billsAccount.accountName = "Bill";
11         billsAccount.balance = 75;
12
13         System.out.println("Freds A/c no: "
14         + fredsAccount.accountNo + " Freds A/c name: "
15         + fredsAccount.accountName + " Freds balance: "
```

```
16              + fredsAccount.balance);
17          System.out.println("Bills A/c no: "
18              + billsAccount.accountNo
19              + " Bills A/c name: " + billsAccount.accountName
20              + " Bills Balance: " + billsAccount.balance);
21   }
22   }
```

When we assign a value of 456 to billsAccount.accountNo, the value of fredsAccount.accountNo is unaffected because Java has created two copies of accountNo corresponding to billsAccount and fredsAccount. The result of executing the program is shown as follows:

```
> java CreateAccount
Freds A/c no: 123 Freds A/c name: Fred Freds Balance: 50.0
Bills A/c no: 456 Bills A/c name: Bill Bills Balance: 75.0
```

A member variable can be defined as a **static** (or **class**) variable by use of the **static** keyword. In this case, a single copy of the member variable is created regardless of the number of instances (even if no instances are created). Each instance has access to the same copy of the static variables. We would make a variable static if it is the same for all objects. For example, we can add the static variable bankName to the Account class definition.

Account—second version

```
1   class Account{
2       static String bankName;
3       int accountNo;
4       String accountName;
5       int balance;
6   }
```

Suppose we add the following statements to the CreateAccount program:

```
fredsAccount.bankName = "Ealing Bank";
billsAccount.bankName = "Kingston Bank";
```

After the second statement is executed, the value of fredsAccount.bankName is also "Kingston Bank" since the billsAccount and fredsAccount objects share the same copy of the bankName variable. Normally, we would not prefix a static variable with an object since it does not make sense to associate a static variable with an object. We prefix static variables with the class name, as follows:

```
Account.bankName = "Ealing Bank";
```

4.7 Instance and Static Methods

As well as instance and static variables, we can also have instance and static (or class) methods. By default, all methods are instance methods. As we have seen in Section 4.2, instance methods are invoked by prefixing the method with an object. For example, we invoke the instance method deposit

```
fredsAccount.deposit(100);
```

The deposit method modifies the instance variables corresponding to the fredsAccount object only.

A static method does not operate on an object. Typically, a method that performs a general-purpose calculation is a candidate for a static method. For example, we will take the Circle application from Chapter 2 and rewrite it as a class containing the calculateArea static method. This returns the area of the circle given a radius as a supplied argument.

Circle—second version

```
1  public class Circle {
2      static final double PI = 3.14159;
3
4      public static double calculateArea (double radius) {
5          // area formula
6          return PI * (radius * radius);
7      }
8  }
```

Circle—second version

Static methods, like static variables, are identified by the use of the static keyword (line 4). We can invoke the calculateArea method from any class by prefixing the method with its class name, for example

```
double circleArea = Circle.calculateArea(5);
```

An instance of the Circle class does not need to exist in order to access the calculateArea static method.

Note that though instance methods can access static variables, static methods cannot access instance variables. An attempt by a static method to access an instance variable will cause a compilation error.

The `java.lang.Math` class, in particular, provides many examples of static methods and constants. These are for use in mathematical calculations and include a more accurate version of `PI` than we used in `Circle`. Consult the Sun API documentation for details.

4.8 this Keyword

In the `Account` class constructor of Section 4.3, we distinguished between member and local variables by giving the variables different identifiers.

```
class Account {
    int accountNo;
    String accountName;
    double balance;

    public Account(int no, String name, double bal){
        accountNo = no;
        accountName = name;
        balance = bal;
    } .......
```

What if we used the same identifiers for member and local variable in the constructor, as follows:

```
public Account(int accountNo, String accountName, double balance) {
    accountNo = accountNo;
    accountName = accountName;
    balance = balance;
}
```

Although this will compile successfully, Java cannot distinguish between the left-side member variables and the right-side local variables. Variables on both sides of the assignment operators are treated as local; the member variables are not set by the constructor. As a result, the value of `fredsAccount.accountNo`, after invoking the constructor in the following code fragment, is 0, the default value for integers in Java, rather than 123.

```
Account fredsAccount = new Account(123, "Fred", 60);
```

To specify an object's member variables, Java provides the **this** keyword, which is prefixed to the member variable or method. The Account class constructor can be written as

```
public Account(int accountNo, String accountName, double balance) {
    this.accountNo = accountNo;
    this.accountName = accountName;
```

```
    this.balance = balance;
}
```

The value of `fredsAccount.accountNo` after invoking the constructor

```
Account fredsAccount = new Account(123, "Fred", 60);
```

is 123 as expected.

`this` is actually a reference to the object being constructed. All object variables are references, so the following code fragment:

```
Account fredsAccount = new Account(...);
Account billsAccount = fredsAccount;
billsAccount.balance = 500;
```

sets the balance for both Bill and Fred.

4.9 StringBuffer

A `StringBuffer` object is similar to a `String` object but is more efficient when you are repeatedly appending characters to a string. Unlike a `String`, a `StringBuffer` is mutable so its contents can be modified. The nonobject-oriented syntactical sugar provided by `String`s in initialization and concatenation does not apply to `StringBuffer` objects. For example, the statement

```
StringBuffer textbuf = "A circle of  ";
```

is illegal. A valid statement would be

```
StringBuffer textbuf = new StringBuffer("A circle of ");
```

The statement

```
textbuf = textbuf + "radius ";
```

is also illegal. We need to make use of the `java.lang.StringBuffer.append` method. The following statement is legal:

```
textbuf.append("radius ");
```

To modify a character within a `StringBuffer` object, use the `java.lang.StringBuffer.setCharAt` method. For example, the statement

```
textbuf.setCharAt(3, 'Z');
```

sets the fourth character (counting starts at zero) of textbuf to 'Z'.

4.10 Vectors

Recall from Chapter 2 that once we create an array we cannot change its size. **Vectors,** on the other hand, can grow and shrink at runtime as required. A Vector is an object of the java.util.Vector class. A Vector object is created using the new keyword, for example,

```
Vector vlist = new Vector();
```

This creates a Vector object, vlist, with default capacity of ten elements. As soon as 10 elements have been added, the capacity, by default, will be doubled to 20 elements in total. It is possible to specify other capacities and increment factors. To add an element to an array, use the java.util.Vector.add method. This method allows you to add any object to the end of the Vector, for example,

```
vlist.add("ABC");
```

adds string "ABC", which is an object, to the end of Vector vlist. The java.util.Vector class provides methods capacity, which returns the current capacity of a Vector, and size, which returns the number of elements in the Vector. There are also methods for returning or deleting elements at a given position in the Vector.

Since Java version 1.2, a Vector is actually an implementation of the List interface, which in turn, is a derivation of the Collection interface. Collections are described in Chapter 9.

Note that a Vector can only hold object types. We cannot directly add a primitive data type, such as int, to a Vector. If we do need to add a primitive to a Vector, we must first convert it to an object using an object wrapper.

4.11 Object Wrappers

Recall that unlike some object-oriented languages, primitive data types are not objects in Java. However, there may be occasions when we need the object equivalents of primitive data types, as we have seen with Vectors. Java provides wrapper classes for this purpose. For example, we cannot directly convert a String, which is an object, into an int primitive; we need to do this directly or indirectly through the int object wrapper Integer. The wrapper classes for equivalent primitive data types are listed in Table 4.1.

Suppose we want to create an Integer object. We can do this like any object using the new keyword, as follows:

```
Integer intObj = new Integer(7);
```

To convert a String to an Integer, use the java.lang.Integer.valueOf method, for example

```
String snum = "456";
Integer intObj = Integer.valueOf(snum);
```

Table 4.1: Object wrappers.

Primitive Data Type	Wrapper Class
byte	java.lang.Byte
short	java.lang.Short
int	java.lang.Integer
long	java.lang.Long
float	java.lang.Float
double	java.lang.Double
boolean	java.lang.Boolean
char	java.lang.Character

To convert an Integer object to an int primitive, we can use the java.lang.Integer.intValue method, for example

```
int count = intObj.intValue();
```

To convert a String to an int primitive, we can perform the previous two statements in one step using the java.lang.Integer.parseInt method, for example

```
int count = Integer.parseInt(snum);
```

chapter 5

Inheritance and Access Control

This chapter concludes discussion of specifically object-oriented features of the Java language. By creating subclasses, we can inherit both variables and methods from other classes; this encourages code reuse. Method overriding is another code reuse feature. Related to the idea of inheritance are the concepts of abstract classes, interfaces, and inner classes. This chapter also discusses packages and access control in Java.

5.1 Creating Subclasses

Inheritance is related to the idea of specializing an existing class. For example, we may wish to create a class SavingsAccount that has all the characteristics of the Account class, shown in Section 4.3, except that a minimum balance has to be present in SavingsAccount.

SavingsAccount

```
1   class SavingsAccount extends Account {
2       double minBalance;
3
4       public SavingsAccount(int no, String name, double balance) {
5           super(no, name, balance);
6           minBalance = 100;
7       }
8
9       public double withdraw(double amount) {
10          if (balance - amount < minBalance) {
11              System.out.println("Insufficient Funds");
12          } else {
13              balance = balance - amount;
14          }
```

```
15          return balance;
16      }
17  }
```

Rather than completely write from scratch all the code for SavingsAccount, we want to reuse as far as possible variables and methods from the Account class. Additionally, we would like to redefine the withdraw method to ensure that the balance does not fall below the required level. The SavingsAccount class is an example of the specialization of the Account class. The SavingsAccount class can be regarded as a subclass of the parent class, or superclass, Account. In Java, the **extends** keyword is used to define a subclass.

The SavingsAccount class inherits both state (variables) and behavior (methods) from the parent Account class. So a SavingsAccount object has a corresponding balance instance variable. SavingsAccount also has an associated deposit method. The withdraw method has been redefined for the SavingsAccount class: this is an example of **method overriding**. Method overriding is another aspect of **polymorphism**. We have also created a constructor for SavingsAccount.

Recall that a constructor has the same identifier as the class to which it belongs. In line 5, the super keyword invokes the parent class constructor. If we leave out this statement, Java automatically invokes the parent constructor with an implied super() statement. Since we do not have a constructor in the Account class without arguments, namely, Account(), we have to explicitly enter the super statement so as to invoke Account(int no, String name, double balance).

CreateSavingsAccount illustrates how we might invoke the SavingsAccount class.

CreateSavingsAccount

```
1   class CreateSavingsAccount {
2
3       public static void main(String[] args) {
4           double balance;
5
6           SavingsAccount fredsAccount =
7                       new SavingsAccount(123, "Fred", 60);
8           fredsAccount.deposit(70);
9           balance = fredsAccount.withdraw(40);
10          balance = fredsAccount.withdraw(20);
11          System.out.println("Balance: " + balance);
12          System.out.println("A/c No: " + fredsAccount.accountNo);
13      }
14  }
```

Note that the statement in line 8 invokes the deposit method inherited from the Account class. The statement in line 9 invokes the overridden withdraw method defined in the SavingsAccount class. Since the remaining balance falls below the minimum balance required, this transaction will fail. The second withdraw method invocation in line 10 does not violate the minimum balance requirement and so succeeds. Note that in line 12 we refer to fredsAccount.accountNo. There is no accountNo instance variable explicitly defined in the SavingsAccount class; this variable has been inherited from the Account class. The following output shows the result of executing the CreateSavingsAccount class:

```
> java CreateSavingsAccount
Insufficient Funds
Balance: 110.0
A/c No: 123
```

In CreateBothAccounts, we create an object fredsAccount of type SavingsAccount if the supplied program parameter is equal to 1; otherwise, we create an object soniasAccount of the parent class type, Account.

CreateBothAccounts

```
1  class CreateBothAccounts {
2
3      public static void main(String[] args) {
4          Account acc;
5          double balance;
6          int arg;
7
8          arg = Integer.parseInt(args[0]);
9          SavingsAccount fredsAccount =
10                     new SavingsAccount(123, "Fred", 120);
11         Account soniasAccount = new Account(456, "Sonia", 120);
12         if (arg == 1) {
13             acc = fredsAccount;
14         } else {
15             acc = soniasAccount;
16         }
17         balance = acc.withdraw(30);
18     }
19 }
```

CreateBothAccounts

We define an acc object of type Account (line 4). This is set to fredsAccount, a child Savings-Account object, if the program parameter is equal to 1 (line 13). Otherwise, acc is set to soniasAccount, a parent Account object (line 15). The crucial line is 17: if the acc object is soniasAccount, the Account withdraw method is invoked, and the resulting balance is 90. If the acc object is fredsAccount, then the overridden SavingsAccount withdraw method is invoked. Since a SavingsAccount requires a minimum balance of 100, the withdrawal is rejected and the balance remains at 120. This ability of an object variable to refer to a class or its subclass is another aspect of polymorphism. Because the decision as to which withdraw method to invoke is made at runtime, and not compile time, it is known as dynamic binding.

We can create chains of inheritance in Java; a subclass will inherit variables and methods explicitly defined in its immediate parent class. Any variables implicitly inherited by the parent class will be also inherited by the subclass. For example, we may want to specialize the SavingsAccount class still further and create a HighInterestSavingsAccount. This class would inherit variables and methods explicitly defined in the SavingsAccount class, namely, the overridden withdraw method. HighInterestSavingsAccount would also inherit the accountNo, accountName, balance variables, and deposit method from the Account class. Of course, any of these can be overridden, in turn, by the HighInterestSavingsAccount class. Note that Java supports only single inheritance; namely, a class can have at most only one direct parent class.

Note that we can declare a method to be **final**: this prevents subclasses from overriding the method. For example,

```
public final double withdraw(double amount) {
```

We can also declare a class to be final if we want to prevent further subclassing. For example,

```
final class SavingsAccount extends Account {
```

We have already used the super keyword to call the parent class constructor. Another use of the super keyword is to invoke any method from the parent class. The syntax for this is super.method_identifier(optional arguments). For example, we can add the deposit method shown next to the SavingsAccount class. This method merely invokes the Account class deposit method, then prints the resulting balance.

deposit Method

```
1  public void deposit(double amount) {
2      super.deposit(amount);
3      System.out.println("New balance: " + balance);
4  }
```

5.1.1   Casting Objects

Consider the following code fragment:

```
Account fredsAccount = new Account(...);
SavingsAccount fredsSavingAccount = new SavingsAccount(...);
fredsAccount = fredsSavingAccount; /* OK */
fredsSavingAccount = fredsAccount;  /* fail */
```

In the first object assignment, the compiler implicitly casts a SavingsAccount type to an Account type. This is done because all instances of SavingsAccount are also instances of Account (upcasting). The second object assignment fails at compilation since we are attempting to implicitly downcast an Account type to a SavingsAccount. Not all instances of Account are also instances of SavingsAccount even though in our example we know that fredsAccount contains an instance of SavingsAccount. We must explicitly downcast, so the following statement would be valid:

```
fredsSavingAccount = (SavingsAccount) fredsAccount;
```

5.2   The Object Class

The Java-supplied java.lang.Object class is the parent or root of all classes. Every class either directly or indirectly is a subclass of the Object class. Whenever we create a class such as

```
class MyClass {
...
}
```

this is implicitly equivalent to

```
class MyClass extends Object {
...
}
```

The Object class contains a number of methods that all classes inherit by default. In many cases, we will need to override these methods within our own classes.

5.2.1   equals Method

We cannot use the logical equality operator, ==, for testing whether two objects are equal since the == operator tests if the two objects are stored in the same memory location. The equals method in the Object class is used to test if the contents of two objects are equal. As an example, let's look at String objects. Consider the following code fragment:

```
String s1 = "abc";
String s2 = new String("abc");
System.out.println(s1 == "abc");
System.out.println(s2 == "abc");
```

Because of String sharing, the first println is likely to output true; however, the second statement will output false. The String class overrides the equals method to return a value of true if the contents of two Strings are equal. So if we replace the println statements with

```
System.out.println(s1.equals("abc"));
System.out.println(s2.equals("abc"));
```

then true will be output in both cases.

What if we have created our own objects and want to test for equality? For example, suppose we have created the following Employee class:

Employee

```
1  class Employee {
2      int empNumber;
3      String name;
4      int salary;
5
6      public Employee(int empNumber, String name, int salary) {
7          this.empNumber = empNumber;
8          this.name = name;
9          this.salary = salary;
10     }
11 }
```

Employee

We create Employee objects, e1 and e2, as follows:

```
Employee e1 = new Employee(1, "Sim", 15000);
Employee e2 = new Employee(1, "Sim", 15000);
```

We want to test if the contents of e1 and e2 are the same. We cannot use the Object.equals method because its default behavior is to act like the == operator. We need to override the equals method so that it acts much like the overridden String.equals method. *The Java Language Specification*[1] states that an overridden equals method must exhibit the following properties:

- It is **reflexive**. For any reference value x, x.equals(x) should return true.

- It is **symmetric**. For any reference values x and y, x.equals(y) should return true if and only if y.equals(x) returns true.

- It is **transitive**. For any reference values x, y, and z, if x.equals(y) returns true and y.equals(z) returns true, then x.equals(z) should return true.

- It is **consistent**. For any reference values x and y, multiple invocations of x.equals(y) consistently return true or consistently return false, provided no information used in equals comparison on the object is modified.

- For any nonnull reference value x, x.equals(null) should return false.

---

[1] J. Gosling et al., *The Java Language Specification 2d ed.* (Boston: Addison-Wesley, 2000).

The preceding properties define an **equivalence relation**. The listing shows an overridden equals method that we might add to the Employee class.

equals Method

```
1  public boolean equals(Object o) {
2      if (o == this) {
3          return true;
4      }
5      if (o == null) {
6          return false;
7      }
8      if (getClass() != o.getClass() ) {
9          return false;
10     }
11     Employee e = (Employee) o;
12     return empNumber == e.empNumber
13             && name.equals(e.name)
14             && salary == e.salary;
15 }
```

equals Method

Lines 2–4 are a check if the argument, o, is a reference to this object. If so, return true. This statement is for efficiency only; it saves the later checking (as in lines 12-14) of the individual fields that could be computationally expensive. In lines 5-7, a null argument fails the equality test in line with the last requirement of the preceding equals equivalence relation. In lines 8-10, we test whether this object and the argument belong to the same class. We use the Object.getClass method, which returns the runtime class of an object. If the two objects do not belong to the same class, they cannot be equal. In line 11, we cast the object argument to an Employee type. Finally, in lines 12-14, we test if the fields of the two objects have identical values. For primitive types, such as the int empNumber and salary, we can safely use the == operator. For the String name, we use the overridden String.equals method.

5.2.2 hashCode Method

The hashCode method in the Object class returns the hash code for the Object. This is an int value that is used as a key when objects are placed in a Hashtable. Hashtables are part of the Collections Framework and are discussed in Chapter 9. Objects that are equal must produce the same hashCode value; otherwise, they will not behave correctly in hash-based Collections. This means that if we override the equals method, as in Employee class, we must also override the `Object` `hashCode` method. We cannot rely on the default `Object` hashCode value. For example, for the following `Employee` objects e1 and e2:

```
Employee e1 = new Employee(1, "Sim", 15000);
Employee e2 = new Employee(1, "Sim", 15000);
```

the values of e1.hashCode() and e2.hashCode() are derived from each instance's memory address and so will not be the same. The listing shows an overridden hashCode method that we might add to the `Employee` class.

hashCode

```
1  public int hashCode() {
2      int result = 17;
3
4      result = 37 * result + empNumber;
5      result = 37 * result + name.hashCode();
6      result = 37 * result + salary;
7      return result;
8  }
```

hashCode

The derivation of the algorithm used in the preceding hashCode method is beyond the scope of this book. It is sufficient to note that we have two main objectives when creating a hashCode method. First, equal objects must have the same hash code. Second, a hash method should distribute unequal instances uniformly across all possible hash values.[2]

5.2.3   toString Method

toString is another method belonging to the `Object` class. The default behavior is to return the name of the class, followed by an @ then the hash code of the object in hexadecimal. toString can be invoked explicitly as in

```
System.out.println(emp2.toString());
```

resulting in something like:

```
Employee@f97
```

toString is also invoked implicitly by Java when concatenating a non-String object with a String, as in

```
System.out.println("emp2 is " + emp2);
```

---

[2] J. Bloch, *Effective Java Programming Language Guide* (Boston: Addison-Wesley, 2001).

resulting in

    emp2 is Employee@f97

Clearly, we would want to override toString in the Employee class to provide more meaningful output. The code shows an overridden toString method that we might add to the Employee class.

toString

```
1  public String toString() {
2      return "Employee[" + empNumber + ", " + name + ", "
3              + salary + "]" ;
4  }
```

toString

The statement

    System.out.println(emp2.toString());

will now output

    Employee[2, Sim, 15000]

5.2.4   instanceof Operator

The instanceof operator is used to check if an object is an instance of the specified class or subclass of that class. If this is the case, instanceof returns the boolean true; otherwise, it returns false. For example, in the code fragment

```
Integer intobj = new Integer(7);
if (intobj instanceof Integer) {
    System.out.println("intobj is an Integer");
}
if (intobj instanceof Object) {
    System.out.println("intobj is an Object");
}
```

since java.lang.Integer is a subclass of java.lang.Object, both if statements are true.

5.3   Abstract Classes and Methods

In our bank account example, we can think of a savings account, checking (or current) account, and long-term deposit account all being physical examples of subclasses of a generalized account class. The account class is generalized, or abstract, in the sense that it makes no sense to have a corresponding instantiated object: whenever a physical account is opened, it must be a savings, checking, or long-term deposit. Nevertheless, we wish to have an account class that will have defined variables and methods common to all subclasses. Such a class is defined using the **abstract** keyword in Java. An abstract class cannot be instantiated. The abstract class can define variables and methods that subclasses can use or, if required, can override.

An abstract class can optionally consist of abstract methods. An abstract method consists of the method declaration only; the method body is omitted. For any subclass of the abstract class, a method must be declared with the same number and types of arguments (or signature) as the abstract method, or the subclass will fail to compile. This is of practical use in large software engineering projects where we want all subclasses of an abstract class to use the same method signature.

The Abstract Account example shows the code for an abstract Account class.

Abstract Account

```
1   abstract class Account {
2
3       int accountNo;
4       String accountName;
5       double balance;
6
7       public Account(int no, String name, double bal){
8           accountNo = no;
9           accountName = name;
10          balance = bal;
11      }
12
13      public abstract void deposit(double amount);
14
15  }
```

Abstract Account

accountNo, accountName, and balance are variables that are inherited by any subclass of Account. Note the abstract class does have a constructor, but it cannot be directly instantiated. We would need to instantiate a subclass, and the subclass constructor would, in turn, invoke the abstract class constructor using the super keyword. deposit is an example of an abstract method. We assume that all subclasses will have a deposit method with one double argument, amount. We assume that not all subclasses will have a withdraw method; LongTermDeposit, for example, may not allow any withdrawals.

CheckingAccount is a subclass of the abstract Account class.

CheckingAccount

```
 1  class CheckingAccount extends Account {
 2
 3      double  minBalance;
 4
 5      public CheckingAccount(int no, String name, double balance) {
 6          super(no, name, balance);
 7          minBalance = 100;
 8      }
 9
10      public void deposit(double amount) {
11          balance = balance + amount;
12      }
13
14      public double withdraw(double amount) {
15          if (balance - amount < 0) {
16              System.out.println("Insufficient Funds");
17          } else {
18              balance = balance - amount;
19          }
20          return balance;
21      }
22  }
```

CheckingAccount

The point to note is that CheckingAccount must contain a public void deposit method with a single double argument since deposit has been defined as an abstract method in the parent abstract Account class. If the deposit method is not present, the CheckingAccount class will not compile.

5.4 Interfaces

An **interface** extends the concept of an abstract class. An interface consists of method declarations; however, no method body is included. An interface is a requirement: it specifies "what" without the "how." The "how" is left to the class that implements the interface. A class that implements an interface undertakes to implement all the methods in the interface. The signatures of the class methods must be the same as those in the interface.

PerformTransaction is an example of an interface with deposit and withdraw method declarations.

PerformTransaction

```
1  interface PerformTransaction {
2      public void deposit (double amount);
3      public double withdraw (double amount);
4  }
```

Note that all methods in an interface are public by default; we have chosen to make this explicit. An interface is not a class, so we do not have a corresponding object. Any class can choose to implement the PerformTransaction interface where it makes sense to have deposit and withdraw methods. To implement an interface, include the implements interface_name keyword in the class declaration, for example,

```
class InvestmentFund implements PerformTransaction {
```

Note that InvestmentFund must include both deposit and withdraw method bodies. The signatures of these methods must match with those in the interface. Failure to comply will cause a compilation error in the InvestmentFund class.

Interfaces provide a form of multiple inheritance since a class can choose to implement any number of interfaces. We shall see examples of this in Chapter 8 when discussing event-handling listener interfaces. Interfaces can include constants as well as methods. For example, we could add the following constants to the PerformTransaction interface:

```
static final int GOOD_CUSTOMER = 1;
static final int BAD_CUSTOMER = 0;
```

It is possible for an interface to define only constants and no methods.

5.5 Packages

Related classes can be grouped in a package. This makes management of large software projects easier. Class name conflicts are reduced. If we are creating a new class, we only need to check that the same class identifier is used in the current package; it does not matter if the same class identifier is used in another package. Packages also provide a mechanism for access control. We can allow classes to have unrestricted access to each other within a package while restricting access to classes outside the package.

The syntax for assigning a class to a package is the statement

```
package  package_identifier;
```

This must be the first statement in the class source code. Suppose we have an Account class, consisting of a constructor, deposit and withdraw methods that we place in the bankaccount package.

```
package bankaccount;
public class Account {
    public Account(...) {...}
    public void deposit(...) {...}
    public double withdraw(...) {...}
}
```

Suppose we create an Account class, consisting of a constructor and a deposit method that belongs to the salesaccount package.

```
package salesaccount;
public class Account {
    public Account(...) {...}
    public void deposit(...) {...}
}
```

The functionality of the class Account in the salesaccount package could be completely different from that of the Account class in the bankaccount package. Note that the source code will be stored in a directory having the same name as the package identifier. For example, on the Windows NT operating system, the two Account classes might be stored in directories

```
C:\JavaSourceCode\bankaccount and
C:\JavaSourceCode\salesaccount
```

In this way, any conflict that would be caused by the rule that the Account class source code must be stored in file Account.java is avoided.

We can also have package hierarchies. For example, we may wish to subdivide the bankaccount package into two subpackages: debit and credit, say. A class that belonged to the debit subpackage would have

```
package bankaccount.debit;
```

as the first statement. The source code would reside in directory

```
C:\JavaSourceCode\bankaccount\debit
```

An application in a package other than bankaccount or salesaccount would access the Account class or methods by prefixing the identifiers with the package name. This is illustrated by the following code fragment

```
bankaccount.Account fredsAccount =
        new bankaccount.Account(123, "Fred", 60);
salesaccount.Account billsAccount =
        new salesaccount.Account(456, "Bill", 70);
```

Of course, if the preceding code fragment belonged in the bankaccount package, then we do not need to use the bankaccount package prefix. The first statement could be rewritten as

```
Account fredsAccount = new Account(123, "Fred", 60);
```

To avoid using the package prefix in a program outside the package being referred to, use the `import` keyword. This must be in a statement that immediately follows any package statement; otherwise, it must be the first statement in the program. For example, the statement

```
import bankaccount.*;
```

allows the program to access any class belonging to the bankaccount package without the bankaccount prefix. We can import individual classes from a package by using the statement

```
import package_identifier.class_identifier;
```

For example,

```
import bankaccount.Account;
```

To achieve global uniqueness, where packages are available to third parties, the following package naming convention is recommended by Sun: Internet domain name in reverse, followed by packages and subpackages. For example, we could have com.sun.java.swing.

One of the strengths of the Java language is the large number of supplied packages and classes. For example, the following packages are included as part of the Java language:

java.awt	Abstract Window Toolkit graphical user interface
java.io	Input and output, covered in Chapter 7
java.sql	JDBC database access

Sun Microsystems also supplies packages that are not strictly part of the Java language. This enables these packages to have releases independently of the language releases. These packages begin with javax. Examples are

javax.swing	Swing graphical user interface, covered in Chapter 8
javax.servlet	Servlets

Details of these packages and many more can be found in the API documentation. The documentation is written in HTML and includes lists of packages and classes as well as an index to all classes, methods, and variables. Numerous HTML links provide cross-referencing: by clicking on a class name, its associated methods are displayed. We can then click on a method name to have details of the method displayed. There are so many supplied classes in Java that programmers should become familiar with the documentation.

5.5.1   classpath Option

At this point, we should mention the `classpath` option of both the `javac` compiler and `java` interpreter. The format is

```
-classpath   path1;path2...
```

This provides a list of starting search directories, which can include jar archive files, searched for classes by tools such as the javac and java. We cover the jar utility in Section 7.7.2. For example, suppose the tool is searching for package1.Class1 and the classpath option, for Windows, is

```
-classpath C:\myjava\myapps;C:\myjava\myjar1.jar
```

For Unix, we would use a colon and forward slashes as separators. The tool would look for Class1 in directory \myjava\myapps\package1 and in myjar1.jar for package1.Class1. javac (but not java) will, by default, also search in the current directory. There is no need to specify search locations for supplied core classes such as java.lang and java.io. The current directory is specified by a dot (.), which is the default if classpath is not specified.

An alternative to using the –classpath option for each application being compiled or interpreted is to set the CLASSPATH environment variable. The details for setting this are operating system dependent; however, the search locations are specified in the same manner as for the –classpath option.

5.6 Access Control

Java allows one to control access to member variables and methods. Java provides the following access levels: **public**, **protected**, **package**, and **private**. public is the most open access level: variables and methods declared public can be accessed by any class. protected is the next level of accessibility: protected variables and methods can be accessed within the same class, package, and subclass, even if the subclass is in a different package. The package, or **friendly**, access level is the default: this allows variables and methods to be accessed from anywhere in the same package. private is the most restrictive access level: private variables and methods can be accessed only in the current class.

In the remainder of this section, we will look at some examples of using access levels. The Private Account example shows an Account class within the bankaccount package. The class member variables all have their access level set to private. The Account constructor has no access level explicitly specified, so the package access level applies by default. We have added a method, balanceCleared, which checks that there is still money in the account. balanceCleared is invoked by the withdraw method. We make balanceCleared private because we may later decide to use a more complex formula for deciding that a balance is clear; one that may involve a different data representation. Consequently, we do not wish to expose balanceCleared to classes other than Account. Another use of private methods is to decompose a large public method into smaller private component methods that on their own make no sense outside the current class.

Private Account

```
1   package bankaccount;
2
3   class Account {
```

```
4        private int accountNo;
5        private double balance;
6        private String accountName;
7
8        Account(int accountNo, String accountName, double balance) {
9            this.accountNo = accountNo;
10           this.accountName = accountName;
11           this.balance = balance;
12       }
13
14       public double withdraw(double amount) {
15           if (balanceCleared(amount)) {
16               balance = balance - amount;
17           } else {
18               System.out.println("Insufficient Funds");
19           }
20           return balance;
21       }
22
23       private boolean balanceCleared(double amount) {
24           if (balance - amount >= 0) {
25               return true;
26           } else {
27               return false;
28           }
29       }
30   }
```

Private Account

Consider the following statements issued from another class in the bankaccount package:

```
Account fredsAccount = new Account(123, "Fred", 60);
if (fredsAccount.balanceCleared(20) )  System.out.println("OK");
fredsAccount.accountName = "FRED";
```

The first statement is legal because the Account constructor has the package access level by default. The second statement is illegal because the balanceCleared method in the Account class has private access level. The third statement is also illegal because the accountName variable is private. A program containing the second and third statements will not compile.

A common strategy is for all instance variables in a class to be declared private; this is known as **encapsulation**. If there is a need for another class to access any of these variables, this can be done through methods that are declared public, protected, or package. For example, in the Account class, we could add the setAccountName method.

```
public void setAccountName(String newName) {
   accountName = newName;
}
```

The advantage of this approach is that we can add a number of data integrity checks within the setAccountName method. For example, if newName contains numeric values or its length is greater than say, 50, the assignment could fail. To use this method, we would replace the illegal statement

```
fredsAccount.accountName = "FRED";
```

with the legal statement

```
fredsAccount.setAccountName("FRED");
```

Similarly, we can create a method, public String getAccountName(), which returns the value of accountName. getAccountName is an example of a **getter**, or **accessor**, method, and by convention, these are prefixed with get. setAccountName is an example of a **setter**, or **mutator**, method, and by convention, these are prefixed with set. These conventions are enforced by environments such as JavaBeans.

The Protected Account example illustrates the use of the protected access level. We revert to the original withdraw method, which checks the balance. Though we are prepared to allow all classes within the bankaccount package and all subclasses of Account to access variables and methods in Account, we are not prepared to expose these to all classes. So we grant all member variables, the constructor, and the withdraw method protected access level. Note the Account class itself has public access level.

Protected Account

```
1   package bankaccount;
2
3   public class Account {
4       protected int accountNo;
5       protected double balance;
6       protected String accountName;
7
8       protected Account(int accountNo, String accountName,
9                         double balance) {
10          this.accountNo = accountNo;
11          this.accountName = accountName;
12          this.balance = balance;
13      }
14
15      protected double withdraw(double amount) {
16          if (balance - amount < 0) {
17              System.out.println("Insufficient Funds");
18          } else {
```

```
19                    balance = balance - amount;
20            }
21            return balance;
22      }
23  }
```

The SubAccount class is a subclass of Account that belongs to the salesaccount package. This subclass does not do very much; it just consists of a constructor that invokes the parent, Account, class constructor using the super keyword.

SubAccount

```
1   package salesaccount;
2
3   import bankaccount.*;
4
5   class SubAccount extends Account {
6       double minBalance;
7
8       SubAccount(int no, String name, double balance) {
9           super(no, name, balance);
10      }
11  }
```

Note that line 5 is legal since the Account class in the Protected Account example was declared public. By default, a class has package access level, which means a subclass can only be created in the same package. Line 9 is also legal since this statement invokes the protected Account constructor in the Account class.

The following statements issued by a program that is within the salesaccount package, but is not a subclass of Account, are all illegal:

```
Account shamsasAccount = new Account(456, "Shamsa", 70);
balance = shamsasAccount.withdraw(10);
shamsasAccount.accountName = "SHAMSA";
```

The first statement is illegal because the Account constructor in the Protected Account example is protected, so it can only be accessed outside the bankaccount package from a subclass of Account. The second statement is illegal because the withdraw method is protected. The third statement is illegal because the accountName variable is protected. Note that the preceding three statements would all be legal if they were placed in the bankaccount package.

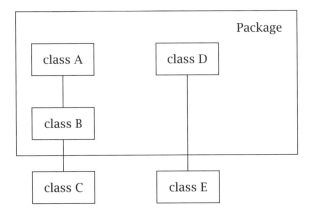

Figure 5.1: Java access levels.

Figure 5.1 summarizes Java access levels. A vertical line represents a subclass relationship, so class B is a subclass of class A. Assume the protection levels are set in class A. Then the following classes can access methods and variables in class A:

public	classes A, B, C, D, and E
protected	classes A, B, C, and D
package, or friendly	classes A, B, and D
private	class A

5.7 Inner Classes

An inner class is a class nested within another class. We can describe an inner class schematically as follows:

```
class Outer {
    class Inner {
        ....
    }
}
```

An inner class has access to member variables of the enclosing, outer, class even if they are declared private. An instance of an inner class can exist only within an instance of the enclosing class. To illustrate this, the Account class includes the Statement inner class.

Account

```
1  public class Account {
2      private int accountNo;
```

```
 3      private String accountName;
 4      private double balance;
 5
 6      public Account(int accountNo, String accountName,
 7                     double balance) {
 8          this.accountNo = accountNo;
 9          this.accountName = accountName;
10          this.balance = balance;
11      }
12
13      public class Statement {
14          private int statementNo;
15
16          public Statement(int statementNo) {
17              this.statementNo = statementNo;
18          }
19
20          public void printStatement() {
21              System.out.println("Account No: " + accountNo);
22              System.out.println("Statement No: " + statementNo);
23              System.out.println("Balance:  " + balance);
24          }
25      }
26  }
```

Account

As before, Account has a constructor (lines 6-11). Lines 13-25 define the Statement inner class. Every Statement has a statement number, and this is initialized in the inner class constructor (lines 16-18). Statement also has a method, printStatement (lines 20-24), that prints account and statement details. Note that accountNo and balance are private variables belonging to the outer, Account, class. Private variables, as we have seen, can normally be accessed only in the current class. However, inner classes are an exception, and we can access accountNo and balance in printStatement.

Note that when we compile the Account.java program, we produce two class files: Account.class and Account$Statement.class. In this way, the one-to-one relationship of class to class file is maintained.

Recall that an inner class instance can exist only within an outer class instance, so the format for creating these instances is

```
OuterClass  OuterClassInstance = new OuterClassConstructor;
OuterClass.InnerClass InnerClassInstance =
          OuterClassInstance.new  InnerClassConstructor;
```

Consequently, the statement

```
Account shamsa = new Account(456, "Shamsa", 500);
```

will create an Account, shamsa, as expected. The statement

```
Account.Statement shamsaStatement = shamsa.new Statement(7);
```

creates shamsaStatement, which is an instance of the inner, Statement, class with a statement number of 7. We cannot create this instance unless the outer class instance, in this case shamsa, is present. We can then invoke an inner class method in the usual way, for example

```
shamsaStatement.printStatement();
```

Inner classes are particularly useful in event-handling applications, for example, when using adapters. In Chapter 8, we discuss Java's event-handling mechanism, including adapters, and provide more examples of inner classes.

Inner classes can be embedded within a method; these are known as **local** inner classes. It is possible to create local inner classes without a name, or **anonymous** inner classes. We shall see an example of this in Chapter 8.

chapter 6

Exceptions

Java provides an exception-handling mechanism that helps you build robust code. When an error occurs at runtime, an exception is thrown. It is possible for an application to catch this exception and, in many cases, recover from it.

6.1 Exception Handling

The Multiply class, which we have seen in Chapter 1, multiplies two integers supplied as arguments and outputs the result.

Multiply

```
 1  public class Multiply {
 2
 3      public static void main(String[] args) {
 4          String resultString;
 5          int arg1;
 6          int arg2;
 7          int result;
 8
 9          arg1 = Integer.parseInt(args[0]);
10          arg2 = Integer.parseInt(args[1]);
11          result = arg1 * arg2;
12          resultString = Integer.toString(result);
13          System.out.println("The product of " + args[0] +
14          " and " + args[1] + " is " + resultString);
15      }
16  }
```

Multiply

If, instead of integers, we supply a real number as an argument, Java will raise the following runtime NumberFormatException:

```
> java Multiply 7.3  8
java.lang.NumberFormatException: 7.3
at java.lang.Integer.parseInt(Integer.java:344)
at java.lang.Integer.parseInt(Integer.java:382)
at Multiply.main(Multiply.java:9)
```

Furthermore, if we were to run the program without supplying any arguments, we would get the following ArrayIndexOutofBoundsException:

```
> java Multiply
java.lang.ArrayIndexOutofBoundsException :   0
at Multiply.main(Multiply.java:9)
```

In both cases, the runtime error is caused when executing the statement in line 9:

```
arg1 = Integer.parseInt(args[0]);
```

The NumberFormatException is caused by attempting to convert a string containing a real number to an integer. The ArrayIndexOutofBoundsException is caused by the size of the args array being zero; consequently, the element args[0] is outside the bounds of the args array.

The try and catch statements allow exceptions to be handled by the program. The try statement contains all the code that may throw an exception. Each exception is handled by a catch statement. When an exception is thrown at runtime, the try block execution is terminated and control is passed to the appropriate catch statement. The form of try and catch statements is

```
try {
    one or more statements that may throw an exception
} catch (Exception e) {
    one or more statements to be executed if this
    exception is thrown
}
```

The second version of Multiply has added exception-handling statements.

Multiply—second version

```
1  public class Multiply {
2
3      public static void main(String[] args) {
4          String resultString;
5          int arg1;
6          int arg2;
7          int result;
8
```

```
 9          try {
10              arg1 = Integer.parseInt(args[0]);
11              arg2 = Integer.parseInt(args[1]);
12              result = arg1 * arg2;
13              resultString = Integer.toString(result);
14              System.out.println("The product of " + args[0]
15              + " and " + args[1] + " is " + resultString);
16          } catch (NumberFormatException e) {
17              System.out.println("Both arguments must be integer");
18          } catch (ArrayIndexOutOfBoundsException e) {
19              System.out.println(
20              "Two integer arguments are required");
21          }
22      }
23  }
```

Multiply—second version

The **finally** statement defines a block of code that is guaranteed to execute after leaving the try block regardless of how we leave it. Consider the following code fragment:

```
try {
    one or more statements that may throw an exception
} catch (Exception1 e) {
    code to execute if Exception1 is thrown, statement a
} catch (Exception2 e) {
    code to execute if Exception2 is thrown, statement b
} finally {
    code guaranteed to execute, statement c
}
next statement, statement d
}
```

If no exception is thrown, then after executing the try block, statements c then d are executed. If either Exception1 or Exception2 are thrown, then either statement a or b will be executed. Control is then passed to statement c, then d. At this point, the finally statement may seem redundant; after all, statement c could be added to the same block as, and immediately prior to, statement d. However, there is a possibility of another runtime exception, Exception3, being thrown. Although we should try to anticipate likely runtime exceptions in our code, it may not be practical to do so. In this case, the program will abort with an error message at some point in the try block before reaching statement d. However, if we have the finally clause in our code, statement c will execute even if Exception3 is thrown before the program aborts. Typically, statement c would contain some sort of tidying-up code. For example, a file may be opened by one of the statements in the try block. The file may still be open when one of the exceptions is thrown. The statement(s) in the `finally` block would close the file if it were still open.

6.2   Java Exception Classes

When an exception is thrown, an object is thrown corresponding to one of the supplied Java exception classes. In Section 6.1, we have seen an example of an exception being thrown by the runtime system; an exception can also be explicitly thrown by the program code. This is illustrated in Section 6.3. Figure 6.1 shows the exception class hierarchy outline.

Note that the `Error` hierarchy describes serious internal errors that applications should not normally try to catch. A large number of exception classes, both runtime and nonruntime, are inherited from the `Exception` class. If you want to know details of any particular exception class, consult the Sun API documentation.

A thrown exception can be caught by an exception class higher in the class hierarchy. For example, lines 18-21 from the `Multiply` example in the previous section,

```
} catch (ArrayIndexOutOfBoundsException e) {
    System.out.println("Two integer arguments are required");
}
```

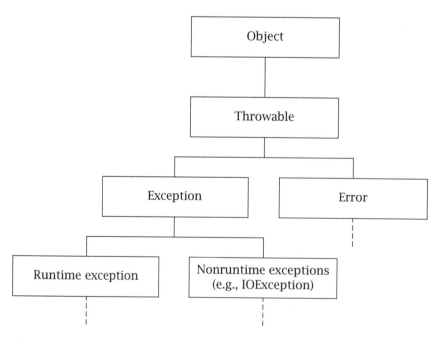

Figure 6.1: Exception hierarchy outline.

could be replaced by

```
} catch (IndexOutOfBoundsException e) {
    System.out.println("Out of Bounds Exception");
}
```

Usually, it is good practice to use the most specific exception class. In the preceding example, the code in the catch statement must be able to handle any possible StringIndexOutOfBounds exceptions as well as ArrayIndexOutOfBounds exceptions.

6.3 Creating Exception Classes

It is possible to create your own exception classes. These exceptions are then explicitly thrown in the program code using the **throw** statement. An exception class is created by creating a subclass of the Java-supplied Exception class. It is possible to create a subclass of a class lower in the exception class hierarchy, for example, a subclass of the RuntimeException class. However, this is not good practice, as we shall see later in this chapter.

As an example, we will create an exception class, ArgumentTooBigException, that catches exceptions thrown whenever arguments supplied to a program exceed a given value.

ArgumentTooBigException

```
1   public class ArgumentTooBigException extends Exception {
2       public ArgumentTooBigException(){}
3   }
```

ArgumentTooBigException

We can use any valid unique identifier for the exception class name. However, the exception class hierarchy in the Java language uses the standard of an exception class ending with the string Exception. It is good practice to continue with this convention, so our class has been named ArgumentTooBigException. It consists of a single constructor that does nothing other than enable the instantiation of the thrown exception object.

Suppose we have a class, MultiplyClass, that consists of single method, multiply, which returns the product of two supplied arguments. If either argument is greater than 99, we want to throw our ArgumentTooBigException.

multiply Method

```
1   public class MultiplyClass {
2
3       public static int multiply(int arg1, int arg2)
4                       throws ArgumentTooBigException {
```

```
 5            if (arg1 > 99 | arg2 > 99) {
 6                throw new ArgumentTooBigException();
 7            }
 8            return arg1 * arg2;
 9        }
10  }
```

Note that in the statement (line 6),

```
throw new ArgumentTooBigException();
```

the new keyword creates a throwable object corresponding to the ArgumentTooBigException class. The throw keyword then throws this object. Note that the method declaration includes the clause throws ArgumentTooBigException (line 4). Java has a requirement that any exception, other than runtime exceptions, must be either caught by the method or specified in the throws clause of the method. Note that a method is not required to declare in its throws clause any subclasses of Error that might be thrown during its execution. Since the multiply method does not catch the exception, it must be specified in the throws clause. Since the exception is part of the method declaration and so part of its interface, any method that invokes the multiply method is aware of the ArgumentTooBig exception, and the invoking method can decide whether to catch the exception.

6.4   Propagation of Exceptions

Continuing with the example of the previous section, suppose MultiplyClass now consists of a main method, which accepts two integer arguments and invokes the multiplyHandler method. multiplyHandler then invokes the multiply method, which as we have seen in the previous section may throw an ArgumentTooBig exception. In this section, we examine how the exception thrown in the multiply method is propagated upwards through the multiplyHandler and main methods.

MultiplyClass

```
 1  public class MultiplyClass {
 2
 3     public static void main(String[] args)
 4                     throws ArgumentTooBigException {
 5        String resultString;
 6        int arg1;
 7        int arg2;
 8        int result;
 9
10        arg1 = Integer.parseInt(args[0]);
```

```
11          arg2 = Integer.parseInt(args[1]);
12          result = multiplyHandler (arg1, arg2);
13          resultString = Integer.toString(result);
14          System.out.println("The product of " + args[0]
15          + " and " + args[1] + " is " + resultString);
16      }
17
18      public static int multiply(int arg1, int arg2)
19                      throws ArgumentTooBigException {
20          if (arg1 > 99 |  arg2 > 99) {
21              throw new ArgumentTooBigException();
22          }
23          return arg1 * arg2;
24      }
25
26      public static int multiplyHandler(int arg1, int arg2)
27                      throws ArgumentTooBigException {
28          return multiply(arg1, arg2);
29      }
30  }
```

MultiplyClass

Since the invoked multiply method specifies the ArgumentTooBigException in its throws clause, this exception must be either caught or specified in the throws clause of the multiplyHandler method. Since multiplyHandler does not catch the exception, we must specify it in the throws clause of the method (line 27).

Now consider the code for the main method. Since the invoked multiplyHandler method specifies ArgumentTooBigException in its throws clause, this exception must be either caught or specified in the throws clause of the main method. Since the main method does not catch the exception, we must specify it in its throws clause (line 4).

Although we have thrown an ArgumentTooBig exception in the multiply method, we have made no attempt to catch the exception using the try catch construct. What happens if the exception is thrown? Java will work through the method call stack, through the multiply, multiplyHandler, and main methods in turn, searching for an exception handler. Since no exception handler is found, the runtime system, and so the Java program, terminates. The following output shows the ArgumentTooBig exception being thrown:

```
> java MultiplyClass 100 98
ArgumentTooBigException
at MultiplyClass.multiply<MultiplyClass.java:29>
at MultiplyClass.multiplyHandler<MultiplyClass.java:23>
at MultiplyClass.main<MultiplyClass.java:13>
```

It is not good practice to throw an exception from the main method and have the runtime system terminate the program. The application should catch the exception and terminate the program in a controlled manner. The second version of MultiplyClass has the main method modified to use the try catch construct.

MultiplyClass—second version

```
1  public class MultiplyClass {
2
3      public static void main(String[] args) {
4          String resultString;
5          int arg1;
6          int arg2;
7          int result;
8
9          try {
10             arg1 = Integer.parseInt(args[0]);
11             arg2 = Integer.parseInt(args[1]);
12             result = multiplyHandler (arg1, arg2);
13             resultString = Integer.toString(result);
14             System.out.println("The product of " + args[0]
15             + " and " + args[1] + " is " + resultString);
16         } catch (ArgumentTooBigException e) {
17             System.out.println("arguments must be < 100");
18             System.out.println(e.toString() );
19         }
20     }
21
22     public static int multiply(int arg1, int arg2)
23                     throws ArgumentTooBigException {
24         if (arg1 > 99 |  arg2 > 99) {
25             throw new ArgumentTooBigException();
26         }
27         return arg1 * arg2;
28     }
29
30     public static int multiplyHandler(int arg1, int arg2)
31                     throws ArgumentTooBigException {
32         return multiply(arg1, arg2);
33     }
34 }
```

MultiplyClass—second version

Recall that the ArgumentTooBig exception must be either caught or specified in the throws clause of the main method. Since the exception is caught, we do not need to specify it in the throws clause.

If we now run `MultiplyClass`, we get the following result:

```
> java MultiplyClass 100 98
arguments must be < 100
ArgumentTooBigException
```

Rather than printing the trace of the method call stack, only the code within the `catch` group of statements is executed.

6.5 Runtime Exceptions

Recall from the previous sections that Java has a requirement that any exception, *other than* **RuntimeException** *or* **Error**, must be either caught by the method or specified in the `throws` clause of the method. Since a runtime exception, as the name suggests, is usually thrown by the runtime system, it may not be practicable for application code to try to catch all such exceptions. For this reason, the requirement to throw or catch runtime exceptions is relaxed by the Java compiler. For example, if instead of an integer, we supply a real number as an argument to the `MultiplyClass` application, the runtime `NumberFormatException` will be thrown. However, there is no requirement to either catch or specify this exception.

This suggests the possibility of subclassing your own exceptions as runtime exceptions. We can rewrite the `ArgumentTooBigException` class as a subclass of `RuntimeException`.

ArgumentTooBigException

```
1  public class ArgumentTooBigException extends
2                                RuntimeException {
3      public ArgumentTooBigException(){}
4  }
```

ArgumentTooBigException

We will now rewrite all the methods of the `MultiplyClass` application without having to either catch or specify the `ArgumentTooBigException`.

MultiplyClass

```
1  public class MultiplyClass {
2
3      public static void main(String[] args){
4          String resultString;
5          int arg1;
6          int arg2;
```

```
 7           int result;
 8
 9           arg1 = Integer.parseInt(args[0]);
10           arg2 = Integer.parseInt(args[1]);
11           result = multiplyHandler (arg1, arg2);
12           resultString = Integer.toString(result);
13           System.out.println("The product of " + args[0]
14           + " and " + args[1] + " is " + resultString);
15   }
16
17       static int multiplyHandler(int arg1, int arg2){
18           return multiply(arg1, arg2);
19       }
20
21       static int multiply(int arg1, int arg2){
22           if (arg1 > 99 |  arg2 > 99) {
23               throw new ArgumentTooBigException();
24           }
25           return arg1 * arg2;
26       }
27   }
```

MultiplyClass

However, this use of runtime exceptions is not good software engineering practice. In the multiply method, we have decided to throw the ArgumentTooBigException. We have also made the decision not to catch this exception in the multiply method. So the decision whether or not to catch the exception is made by the invoking method, multiplyHandler. The only way the developer of the multiplyHandler method knows which exceptions he or she may need to catch is by examining the code of multiply to see what exceptions are thrown. On a large project, multiplyHandler and multiply may be developed by separate teams. The multiply method may be part of a general utilities class, which may be invoked by a large number of different methods. In all the preceding scenarios, we would not want users of the multiply method to have to trawl through our code. All this violates the principle of information hiding; namely, the invoker of any method needs only to be aware of the method interface but not details of the invoked method body. Consequently, it is good practice to create your own exceptions as subclasses of the Exception class. In this way, the catch or specify exceptions requirement is enforced.

6.6 Assertions

The **assert** statement, introduced in J2SE 1.4, consists of a boolean expression the programmer believes to be true when it is executed. If it is not true, Java will throw an

AssertionError exception. Assertions are useful in testing and debugging programs. The syntax for assert is

```
assert  boolean expression;
```

If boolean expression evaluates to false, an AssertionError exception is thrown with no associated message. Alternatively, we can use the syntax

```
assert boolean expression :  value expression;
```

where value expression is an expression that returns a value; the string equivalent of this value is output in the AssertionError message if boolean expression is false.

Assertions are typically used within a default else clause, within an if/else statement, or within a switch statement with no default case. For example, suppose TestAssert contains the following code fragment:

```
switch (x) {
case 1:
    System.out.println("case 1");
    break;
case 2:
    System.out.println("case 2");
    break;
default:
    assert false : x;
    System.out.println("default");
    break;
}
System.out.println("carry on");
```

We believe that x can take on only the values 1 or 2. Should x take on any other value, the assert will fail.

By default, the javac compiler runs in 1.3 compatibility mode, so the -source option should be used, as follows:

```
> javac -source 1.4 TestAssert.java
```

At runtime, assertion checking is disabled by default. So if x is equal to 3, say, we will get the following result:

```
> java TestAssert
default
carry on
```

To enable runtime assertion checking, use the -ea option, as follows:

```
> java -ea TestAssert
Exception in thread "main" java.lang.AssertionError: 3
        at TestAssert.main(TestAssert.java:12)
```

chapter 7

Input/Output

Input and output are performed in Java by means of streams. The same mechanism is used whether the information is being input or output by means of a file, terminal I/O, socket, or pipe. Separate streams are used for reading from a source and for writing to a destination or sink. For both these streams, the mechanism is open a stream, read or write information, and close the stream. The java.io package provides a large number of classes to handle the different physical I/O implementations. These are shown in Figures 7.1 to 7.4. J2SE 1.4 includes the java.nio, or "New I/O," package. This supplements the existing java.io package and contains features such as buffering for primitive data types and mapping a file in memory. These subjects are beyond the scope of this book; in this chapter, we cover the java.io package.

At the top level are InputStream and OutputStream. InputStream is an abstract class representing an input stream of bytes. This class has a number of methods, the most important of which are a number of overloaded read methods. OutputStream is an abstract class representing a output stream of bytes. This class has a number of methods, the most important of which are a number of overloaded write methods. A number of specialized classes are inherited from InputStream and OutputStream that override their parent methods to handle specific I/O implementations, for example, files or pipes. Figures 7.1 and 7.2 also show a number of subclasses of FilterInputStream and FilterOutputStream. These filter streams add functionality to existing streams, for example, providing buffering or letting an application read or write primitive Java data types. We will see examples of these streams later in this chapter.

Similar to InputStream and OutputStream classes are the Reader and Writer classes. However, these are abstract classes that represent input and output streams of characters rather than bytes.

We will cover only some of the I/O streams and for each stream one or two methods. If you want to know more about any stream, consult the Sun API documentation.

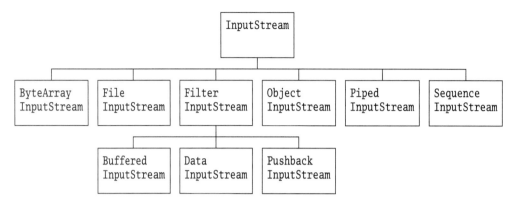

Figure 7.1: InputStream hierarchy.

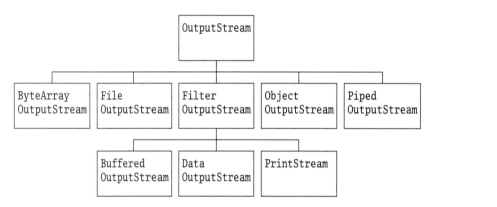

Figure 7.2: OutputStream hierarchy.

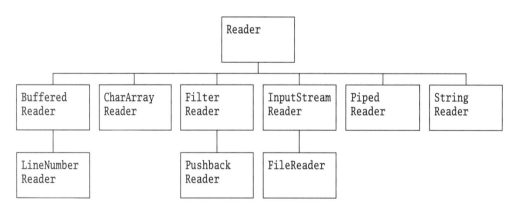

Figure 7.3: Reader hierarchy.

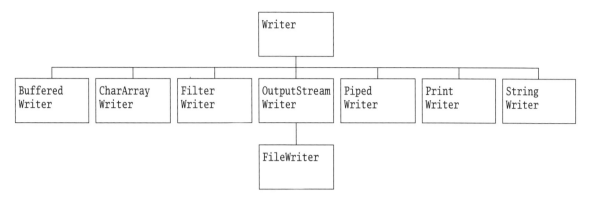

Figure 7.4: Writer hierarchy.

7.1 Terminal I/O Example

To illustrate the use of InputStreams and OutputStreams, Terminal reads in a stream of bytes from the standard input, typically a computer keyboard, and displays the result to the standard output, typically a computer screen.

Terminal

```
1   import java.io.*;
2
3   public class Terminal {
4
5       public static void main(String[] args) throws IOException {
6           int b;
7
8           while ((b = System.in.read() ) != -1) {
9               System.out.print((char)b);
10          }
11      }
12  }
```

Terminal

In line 1, we use the import statement to abbreviate java.io class names. In line 8, note that java.lang.System.in is the standard input. This is an InputStream object. So we can use one of the overloaded read methods from the InputStream class. This returns a byte, b, of type int. The value −1 is returned by read when the end of the stream is reached. The read method throws an IOException, so we need the throws clause in the declaration of line 5. In line 9, we output to the standard output, java.lang.System.out. This is not actually an OutputStream object but a PrintStream object (PrintStream being a subclass of OutputStream). So we can use one of the overloaded print methods of the PrintStream class to print out b, having first cast it to a character.

7.2   FileReader and FileWriter Streams

FileReader and FileWriter are character streams, belonging to the Reader and Writer hierarchies, that are specialized for performing file input and output. These streams handle 16-bit Unicode characters, and so would normally be used when handling files containing textual data. Java also provides equivalent byte streams, FileInputStream and FileOutputStream, that handle ISO-Latin-1 8-bit bytes. Typically, these streams would be used for handling image and sound data.

Java provides a class, java.io.File, for representing files. The constructor File(filename) creates a file instance. filename is a string containing just the file name or the full directory path name; for example, File1.txt or \\MyJavaFiles\\File1.txt on Windows. In the former case, the physical file will reside in the same directory as the Java program accessing the file. Note the use of double backslash characters in the Windows path name, since a single backslash is the escape character within a string. You can use a single forward slash, for example, /MyJavaFiles/File1.txt, for both Windows and Unix directory paths. To ensure portability beyond Windows or Unix environments, the java.io.File class provides a separator static variable that provides the file separator for the local host.

A number of methods in the File class provide information about the properties or existence of files. For example, the method File.exists() returns the boolean true if the specified file physically exists.

To open a file for reading, we create a FileReader object on the file. Either a string or file object should be supplied to the FileReader constructor. There are a number of methods in the java.io.FileReader class, the most useful being read. This method is overloaded to take a string, a single character, or an array of characters as arguments.

To open a file for writing, we create a FileWriter object on the file. Again, either a string or file object should be supplied to the FileWriter constructor. There are a number of methods in the java.io.FileWriter class, the most useful being write. This method is overloaded to take a string, a single character, or an array of characters as arguments.

7.2.1   FileWriter Example

The WriteFile example writes ten lines of text to a file, File1.txt.

WriteFile

```
1  import java.io.*;
2
3  public class WriteFile {
```

```
4
5      public static void main(String[] args) throws
6                                    IOException{
7          String text;
8          int i;
9
10         File outputFile = new File("File1.txt");
11         FileWriter out = new FileWriter(outputFile);
12         for (i=1; i<11; i++) {
13             text = "Line " + i + " of text\n";
14             out.write(text);
15         }
16         out.close();
17     }
18  }
```

WriteFile

As the FileWriter write method throws an IOException, we include the clause throws IOException in the main declaration (lines 5-6). Line 10 creates a file object, outputFile, associated with the physical file File1.txt. In line 11, this file object is then passed as an argument to the FileWriter constructor, which creates an output stream, out. We could have omitted creating the file object and passed the file name as an argument to the FileWriter constructor, as follows:

```
FileWriter out = new FileWriter("File1.txt");
```

In lines 12-15, we have a for loop that, for each of ten iterations, creates a line of text held in the string variable, text. In line 13, note that the last character in the string is \n; this creates a new line after the string has been output. In line 14, the text is output to the file using the java.io.FileWriter.write method.

Finally, in line 16, we use the java.io.FileWriter.close method to close the output stream and release associated system resources. We do not have to explicitly close the output stream; it is implicitly closed by the Java garbage collector when the output stream object is no longer referenced. However, it is good practice to explicitly close streams when they are no longer needed.

7.2.2   The write Method

We mentioned earlier that the java.io.FileWriter.write method is overloaded to take either a string, a single character, or an array of characters as an argument. The WriteFile example used a string, text, as an argument to the write method. The second version of WriteFile has the same functionality as before, except that it converts the output string to a char array, charbuff, then uses charbuff as an argument to the write method.

WriteFile—second version

```
1   import java.io.*;
2
3   public class WriteFile {
4
5       public static void main(String[] args) throws
6                                       IOException{
7           String text;
8           char charbuff[] = new char [30];
9           int i;
10          int j;
11
12          FileWriter out = new FileWriter("File1.txt");
13          for (i=1; i<11; i++) {
14              text = "Line " + i + " of text\n";
15              for (j=0; j < text.length(); j++) {
16                  charbuff[j] = text.charAt(j);
17              }
18              out.write(charbuff, 0 ,text.length() );
19          }
20          out.close();
21      }
```

WriteFile—second version

The char array is created in line 8. We have dispensed with creating a file object; instead, in line 12, we supply the file name as an argument to the FileWriter constructor.

In lines 15-17, we have a for loop that takes each character in a string, converts it to a type char, and assigns it to the charbuff array. The method java.langString.charAt(j) takes the jth character of the supplied string and returns a char value.

In line 18, we use the write(char Array, offset, length) form of the write method to output charbuff to the output stream, out.

7.2.3   The OutputStreamWriter Stream

The observant reader will have noticed in Figure 7.4 that FileWriter is a subclass of OutputStreamWriter. The OutputStreamWriter stream converts characters written to it to bytes: OutputStreamWriter can be wrapped around any byte OutputStream, including File-OutputStream. FileWriter is actually a convenience class that is equivalent to an Output-StreamWriter stream wrapped around a FileOutputStream. So the statement in line 12 of WriteFile,

```
    FileWriter out = new FileWriter("File1.txt");
```

is equivalent to

```
FileOutputStream fout = new FileOutputStream("File1.txt");
OutputStreamWriter out = new OutputStreamWriter(fout);
```

Characters written to an OutputStreamWriter are converted to bytes using a character encoding scheme. The default is the host's default encoding scheme. For Windows, this is ISO 8859-1, the ISO Latin alphabet No. 1. To use another encoding scheme, it has to be specified in the second form of the OutputStreamWriter constructor. For example, if we want to specify the ISO 8859-7 Latin/Greek alphabet, we would use the constructor

```
OutputStreamWriter out = new
                    OutputStreamWriter(fout, "ISO8859_7");
```

7.2.4 The PrintWriter Stream

The PrintWriter stream is used for printing strings and numbers in text format. A PrintWriter stream can be wrapped around any byte OutputStream or character Writer stream, including FileWriter. The PrintWriter class implements all the print methods of the PrintStream class. The WritePrintFile program has the same functionality as the WriteFile program from Section 7.2.1, but outputs to a PrintWriter wrapped around a FileWriter stream.

WritePrintFile

```
1   import java.io.*;
2
3   public class WritePrintFile {
4
5       public static void main(String[] args) throws
6                                           IOException{
7           String text;
8           int i;
9
10          File outputFile = new File("File1.txt");
11          FileWriter out = new FileWriter(outputFile);
12          PrintWriter p = new PrintWriter(out);
13          for (i=1; i<11; i++) {
14              p.println("Line " + i + " of text");
15          }
16          p.close();
17          out.close();
18      }
19  }
```

In lines 10-12, we create a PrintWriter object, p, wrapped around the FileWriter stream, out, which outputs to our file File1.txt. Note in line 14, we use the PrintWriter println method, which prints the string then terminates the line, so dispensing with the \n newline character.

7.2.5   FileReader Example

The ReadFile example reads a file, File1.txt, and prints out the contents of the file to the standard output stream using the System.out.print method.

ReadFile

```
 1  import java.io.*;
 2
 3  public class ReadFile {
 4
 5      public static void main(String[] args) throws
 6                                    IOException {
 7          File inputFile = new File("File1.txt");
 8          if ( ! inputFile.exists() ) {
 9              System.out.println("File does not exist");
10              System.exit(1);
11          }
12          FileReader in = new FileReader(inputFile);
13          int c;
14          while ((c = in.read()) != -1){
15              System.out.print( (char) c );
16          }
17          in.close();
18      }
19  }
```

ReadFile

In line 7, we create a file object, inputFile, using the java.io.File constructor. In line 8, we test the physical existence of this file using the java.io.File.exists method. If the file does not exist, the program prints a message, then terminates using the System.exit method (lines 9-10).

If the file does exist, we then create an input stream, in, with the java.io.FileReader constructor (line 12). In line 14, we use the java.io.FileReader.read method to read a single character from the input stream. This method returns a value of −1 when the end of the input stream is reached. Consequently, the while statement will read all the characters in turn from the input stream. The read method returns a character, c, of type int, so we need to cast this to a char type to use the System.out.print method in line 15.

Analogous to FileWriter, FileReader is actually a convenience class that is equivalent to an InputStreamReader stream wrapped around a FileInputStream. So the statement in line 12 of ReadFile,

```
FileReader in = new FileReader(inputFile);
```

is equivalent to

```
FileInputStream fin = new FileInputStream(inputFile);
InputStreamReader in = new InputStreamReader(fin);
```

Like OutputStreamWriter, InputStreamReader also has a constructor for specifying non-default character-encoding schemes.

7.2.6   Using FileNotFoundException

The ReadFile example in the previous section used the java.io.File.exists method to test for the existence of the input file, and aborting with an error message if the file was not present. The second version of ReadFile achieves the same functionality by testing for a FileNotFoundException using try catch statements.

ReadFile—second version

```
1   import java.io.*;
2
3   public class ReadFile {
4
5       public static void main(String[] args) throws
6                                       IOException {
7           File inputFile = new File("File1.txt");
8           try {
9               FileReader in = new FileReader(inputFile);
10              int c;
11              while ((c = in.read()) != -1){
12                  System.out.print( (char) c );
13              }
14              in.close();
15          } catch (FileNotFoundException e) {
16              System.out.println("File does not exist");
17              System.exit(1);
18          }
19      }
20  }
```

ReadFile—second version

Most of the program's processing is within the try statement. In line 9, if the file
File1.txt does not physically exist, then the java.io.FileReader constructor will raise a
FileNotFoundException. This exception is handled by the catch statement in line 15. In
this case, the program prints a message, then terminates using the System.exit method
(lines 16–17).

7.3   FileInputStream and FileOutputStream

The FileReader and FileWriter streams handle 16-bit Unicode characters, so would normally
be used when handling files containing textual data. The equivalent byte streams, File-
InputStream and FileOutputStream, handle ISO-Latin 8-bit bytes. Typically, these streams would
be used for handling image and sound data. The ReadWriteFile example reads the contents of
file File1.txt using FileInputStream and writes them to File2.txt using FileOutputStream.

ReadWriteFile

```
1   import java.io.*;
2
3   public class ReadWriteFile {
4
5       public static void main(String[] args) throws
6                                       IOException {
7           int c;
8
9           File inputFile = new File("File1.txt");
10          File outputFile = new File("File2.txt");
11          FileInputStream in = new FileInputStream(inputFile);
12          FileOutputStream out =
13                          new FileOutputStream(outputFile);
14          while ((c = in.read()) != -1){
15              out.write(c);
16          }
17          in.close();
18          out.close();
19      }
20  }
```

In lines 9–10, we create file objects, inputFile and outputFile. In lines 11–13, we then
use FileInputStream and FileOutputStream constructors to create the two stream objects,
in and out. Line 14 uses the java.io.FileInputStream.read method in the same way as the
java.io.FileReader.read method described in Section 7.2.5. Most of the methods in the

FileReader and FileWriter classes have an equivalent in FileInputStream and FileOutput-Stream, respectively.

Line 15 uses the form of the java.io.FileOutputStream.write method that outputs a single character, c, at a time to the output stream, out.

7.4   Buffered Input and Output Streams

If a large amount of data is being read from a source or written to a destination, buffering will make the processing more efficient. Instead of accessing the destination for every write, by using a buffered output stream, data is written to a buffer; when the buffer is full, it is sent to the destination with one write. Similarly, with a buffered read operation, the buffer is filled with a single read. If the stream is a file stream, then both the source and destination will typically be a disk file. Buffered streams are used in conjunction with character or byte streams. BufferedReader and BufferedWriter are buffered streams used to wrap any character Reader or Writer stream; for file streams, these are FileReader and FileWriter, respectively. BufferedInputStream and BufferedOutputStream are buffered streams used to wrap any byte InputStream or OutputStream; for file streams, these are FileInputStream and FileOutputStream, respectively.

When creating a buffered stream using the buffered stream constructor, you can specify a buffer size or use the default size.

The following sections illustrate the BufferedReader and BufferedWriter streams. BufferedInputStream and BufferedOutputStream are handled in a similar manner, so we have not shown any examples of these.

7.4.1   BufferedWriter Example

Recall the WriteFile example, from Section 7.2.1, which uses the FileWriter stream to write ten lines of text to file File1.txt. We have modified this to use a BufferedWriter stream; the result is WriteBufFile.

WriteBufFile

```
1   import java.io.*;
2
3   public class WriteBufFile {
4
5       public static void main(String[] args) throws
6                                       IOException{
7           String text;
8           int i;
9
10          FileWriter out = new FileWriter("File1.txt");
11          BufferedWriter outBuffer = new BufferedWriter(out);
12          for (i = 1; i < 11; i++) {
```

```
13                text = "Line " + i + " of text\n";
14                outBuffer.write(text);
15            }
16            outBuffer.close();
17            out.close();
18        }
19 }
```

In line 10, we create a `FileWriter` stream as previously. In line 11, we create a `BufferedWriter` stream with the default buffer size to wrap the `FileWriter` stream, `out`.

The remaining code is as before except that in line 14 we write to the buffer stream using the `java.io.BufferedWriter.write` method.

7.4.2   Flushing the BufferedWriter Stream

When data is being written using `BufferedWriter`, unless the total data is an exact multiple of the buffer size, some data will be left in the buffer that has not been written to the destination. Normally, this is not a problem because as soon as the `BufferedWriter` stream is closed, either explicitly or implicitly when the program terminates, the buffer is implicitly flushed, that is, the remaining buffer contents are written to the destination.

However, there may be occasions when we want to explicitly flush the buffer. To do this, use the `java.io.BufferedWriter.flush` method. For example, in the `WriteBufFile` example of the previous section, we add the statement

```
outBuffer.flush();
```

immediately before closing the `BufferedWriter` stream (line 17) to explicitly flush the buffer.

7.4.3   BufferedReader Example

Recall the `ReadFile` example from Section 7.2.5 that uses the `FileReader` stream to read and print the contents of file `File1.txt`. We have modified this to use a `BufferedReader` stream; the result is `ReadBufFile`.

ReadBufFile

```
1  import java.io.*;
2
3  public class ReadBufFile {
4
5      public static void main(String[] args) throws
6                                      IOException {
7          int c;
```

```
 8
 9          FileReader in = new FileReader("File1.txt");
10          BufferedReader inBuffer = new BufferedReader(in);
11          while ((c = inBuffer.read()) != -1){
12              System.out.print( (char) c );
13          }
14          inBuffer.close();
15          in.close();
16      }
17  }
```

ReadBufFile

In line 9, we create a FileReader stream as previously. In line 10, we then create BufferedReader stream to wrap the FileReader stream, in.

The remaining code is as before except that in line 11 we read from the buffer stream using the java.io.BufferedReader.read method.

7.5 DataInputStream and DataOutputStream

DataInputStream and DataOutputStream are streams that enable applications to read or write primitive Java data types by wrapping an underlying byte stream. For file streams, these underlying streams are FileInputStream and FileOutputStream. Both the java.io.DataInputStream and java.io.DataOutputStream classes contain a large number of methods for reading and writing the primitive Java data types. DataInputStream and DataOutputStream are examples of filter streams.

7.5.1 DataOutputStream Example

The WriteBinFile example writes out an order to a file File1.dat. The order consists of a number of lines; each line is made up of an item, price, and quantity ordered as follows:

```
ice axe;74.99;2
crampons;44.95;1
sleeping bag;100.00;1
mittens;37.50;3
```

A semicolon is used as a field separator.

WriteBinFile

```
1  import java.io.*;
2
3  public class WriteBinFile {
```

```
 4
 5     public static void main(String[] args) throws
 6                                      IOException {
 7        FileOutputStream fileOut = new
 8                        FileOutputStream("File1.dat");
 9        DataOutputStream out = new DataOutputStream(fileOut);
10        String[] item = {"ice axe", "crampons",
11                        "sleeping bag", "mittens"};
12        float[] price = {74.99f, 44.95f, 100.00f, 37.50f};
13        int[] qty = {2, 1, 1, 3};
14        char fieldSeparator = ';';
15        char lineSeparator = '\n';
16        int i;
17        for (i = 0; i < 4; i++) {
18            out.writeChars(item[i]);
19            out.writeChar(fieldSeparator);
20            out.writeFloat(price[i]);
21            out.writeChar(fieldSeparator);
22            out.writeInt(qty[i]);
23            out.writeChar(lineSeparator);
24        }
25        out.close();
26     }
27  }
```

WriteBinFile

In lines 7-8, we create a FileOutputStream object, fileOut, in the usual way.

In line 9, we use the DataOutputStream constructor to create an object, out, to wrap the FileOutputStream, fileOut.

In lines 10-13, we create a String array, item, holding the four items, a float array, price, holding the four prices, and an int array, qty, holding the four quantities. In lines 14-15, we define field and line separators.

In lines 17-24, we use a for loop to output the four lines to the DataOutputStream. For each line, we use the following methods from the java.io.DataOutputStream class:

writeChars	outputs a String data type, in this case, item
writeChar	outputs a char data type, in this case, the field separator
writeFloat	outputs a float data type, in this case, price
writeChar	outputs another field separator
writeInt	outputs an int data type, in this case, qty
writeChar	outputs the line separator

7.5.2 DataInputStream Example

The ReadBinFile example reads the file File1.dat, produced by WriteBinFile described in the previous section, and prints the file contents.

ReadBinFile

```
1   import java.io.*;
2
3   public class ReadBinFile {
4
5       public static void main(String[] args) throws
6                                           IOException {
7           float price;
8           int qty;
9           char singlechar;
10          StringBuffer item;
11          FileInputStream fileIn = new FileInputStream("File1.dat");
12          DataInputStream in = new DataInputStream(fileIn);
13          try {
14              while (true) {
15                  item = new StringBuffer(30);
16                  while ((singlechar = in.readChar()) != ';') {
17                      item.append(singlechar);
18                  }
19                  price = in.readFloat();
20                  in.readChar();     /* skip field separator */
21                  qty = in.readInt();
22                  in.readChar();     /* skip line separator */
23                  System.out.println("item: " + item + " price: "
24                  + price + " quantity: " + qty);
25              }
26          } catch (EOFException e) {
27              in.close();
28          }
29      }
30  }
```

ReadBinFile

In line 11, we create a FileInputStream object, fileIn, in the usual way. In line 12, we use the DataInputStream constructor to create an object, in, to wrap the FileInputStream, fileIn.

With a DataInputStream, we cannot use −1 to indicate we have reached the end of a file. Instead, we use try catch statements that handle the EOFException that is raised when any of the `DataInputStream` read methods reach the end of the file. Within the `try` statement, we start an infinite loop in line 14.

In lines 15–18, we use the `DataInputStream.readChar` method to read a single character, `singlechar`, from the stream. Each character is appended to the variable `item`, a `StringBuffer` data type, until we read a field separator.

In line 19, we read the price from the stream using the `DataInputStream.readFloat` method. We use the `readChar` method to skip the field separator (line 20), then read the quantity using the `readInt` method (line 21). We use the `readChar` method again to skip the line separator (line 22), then in lines 23–24 print the file contents for the current line to the standard output stream.

7.5.3 Wrapping Filter Streams

Filter streams can be successively layered. For example, in the `WriteBinFile` program of Section 7.5.1, we could use a buffered `DataOutputStream` with the statements

```
FileOutputStream fileOut = new FileOutputStream("File1.dat");
BufferedOutputStream buffOut = new BufferedOutputStream(fileOut);
DataOutputStream out = new DataOutputStream(buffOut);
```

7.6 Random Access Files

All the file input and output streams discussed so far in this chapter are sequential. This is fine for batch processing, where the entire contents of a file are either read, written to, or updated. However, this sequential mode can be very inefficient when we want to access just a few records in a large file stored on disk. If the record is located at the beginning of the file, there will be little degradation in performance; if the record is located at the end of the file, we will need to read through the entire file to reach our desired record. Random access provides nonsequential or direct access to the contents of a file. In Java, this facility is achieved by maintaining an index or file pointer. The file pointer is moved whenever data is read from or written to the file and so provides the current position in the file.

Java provides the `java.io.RandomAccessFile` class both for reading from and writing to random access files. The class provides a number of methods, many of which are similar to the read and write methods we have seen for other streams. However, a few methods are unique to this class; the most significant are `getFilePointer` and `seek`. `getFilePointer` returns the current position of the file pointer; `seek` positions the file pointer just before the specified byte offset.

This means that to randomly access a record, we need to know its position in the file. Consequently, although variable length records are permitted in Java random access files, they are most likely to be of fixed length. Also in practice, we would need an algorithm that would map a record's unique key identifier to a byte offset position in the file.

7.6.1 Writing to a Random Access File

The WriteRAF example writes ten records to a random access file RAFile1.dat. Obviously, in practice, we would use a random access for files of at least several thousand records. Each record consists of a string corresponding to a person's address. Random access records can consist of fields corresponding to any of the Java primitive data types.

WriteRAF

```
1   import java.io.*;
2
3   public class WriteRAF {
4
5       public static void main(String[] args) throws
6                                       IOException {
7           int i;
8           String text;
9           RandomAccessFile fileOut;
10
11          fileOut = new RandomAccessFile("RAFile1.dat", "rw");
12          for (i=1; i<11; i++) {
13              text = "Address of " + i + " person\n";
14              System.out.println("offset: " + fileOut.length() );
15              fileOut.seek(fileOut.length() );
16              fileOut.writeChars(text);
17          }
18          fileOut.close();
19      }
20  }
```

WriteRAF

In line 11, we create a random access file object, fileOut, which corresponds to physical file RAFile1.dat using the RandomAccessFile constructor. When creating a random access file, we need to specify whether the file is for reading and writing, "rw", or for reading only, "r".

We execute a for loop (lines 12-17) that writes each record to the file. In line 15, we position the file pointer at the end of the file so that we append the records to the file in the right order. The java.io.RandomAccessFile.length method returns the length, in bytes, of the file. We then use this length as the offset argument in the java.io.RandomAccess.seek method. Because each string is 20 characters, or 40 bytes, in length, we know the offsets for each record will be 0, 40, 80, 120, and so on. The println statement in line 14 simply confirms this.

In line 16, we use RandomAccessFile.writeChars to write the address string, text, as a sequence of characters to the file.

7.6.2 Reading from a Random Access File

The ReadRAF example reads the random access file, RAFile1.dat, created in the previous section. We retrieve the record identified by an offset of 80 bytes, the third record, and print its contents to the standard output stream.

ReadRAF

```
1   import java.io.*;
2
3   public class ReadRAF {
4
5       public static void main(String[] args) throws
6                                       IOException {
7           char singlechar;
8           StringBuffer address;
9           RandomAccessFile fileIn;
10
11          fileIn = new RandomAccessFile("RAFile1.dat", "r");
12          fileIn.seek(80);
13          address = new StringBuffer(20);
14          while ((singlechar = fileIn.readChar()) != '\n') {
15              address.append(singlechar);
16          }
17          System.out.println(address);
18          fileIn.close();
19      }
20  }
```

In line 11, we use the RandomAccessFile constructor to create our file object, fileIn, only this time we specify a read-only file. If we attempt to write to this file with any of the write methods, an IOException will be thrown.

In line 12, we position the file pointer at an offset of 80 bytes using the java.io.Random-AccessFile.seek method.

In lines 14–16, we have a while loop that reads each single character from the file and appends to a StringBuffer variable, address. The while loop is terminated when we read the line separator. The single characters are read from the file using the java.io.RandomAccess-File.readChar method. The record contents, which are now held in the address variable, are printed to the standard output stream in line 17.

7.7 Object Serialization

Normally, objects do not persist beyond the lifetime of the program that created them. However, persistence is required when we write objects to a file to be later read back in, possibly by a different program. Although we have seen how to read and write primitive data types and text to a file, we require a mechanism for storing the state of an object. Serialization converts an object and its state to a stream of bytes. RMI (Remote Method Invocation) also uses serialization to transparently communicate with objects on remote machines.

The JVM automatically handles most details of serialization, at least for default cases. However, Java provides a mechanism where we can customize the serialization process if required.

Serialization is a large topic, and we cover just the basics here. Topics such as class versioning, or evolution, have been omitted.

The byte streams ObjectInputStream and ObjectOutputStream allow us to read and write objects. As an example, consider the following Account class. Account includes a constructor that throws a customized ValueTooSmallException if we attempt to create an Account object with a negative balance.

ValueTooSmallException

```
1  public class ValueTooSmallException extends
2                                    Exception {
3      public ValueTooSmallException(){}
4
5      public ValueTooSmallException(String message) {
6          super(message);
7      }
8  }
```

ValueTooSmallException

Account

```
1  import java.io.*;
2
3  class Account implements Serializable {
4      int accountNo;
5      String accountName;
6      double balance;
7
8      Account(int accountNo, String accountName, double balance)
9                              throws ValueTooSmallException {
10         this.accountNo = accountNo;
11         this.accountName = accountName;
```

```
12              if (balance < 0) {
13                  throw new ValueTooSmallException("Negative Balance");
14              } else {
15                  this.balance = balance;
16              }
17        }
18  }
```

Suppose we want to write Account objects to a file and subsequently read these from the file. The first requirement for writing an object to a stream is that the corresponding class must implement the Serializable interface. So note the implements Serializable clause in line 3. Note that the Serializable interface does not require us to implement any methods. Such a no-method interface is known as a **marker** interface.

A second requirement is that the object's member variables are nonstatic. Serialization will not affect static variables; they may be different when the object is read back in, or deserialized.

WriteAccount is a program that writes two Account objects, account1 and account2, to a file acc.dat.

WriteAccount

```
1  import java.io.*;
2
3  class WriteAccount {
4
5      public static void main(String[] args) throws
6                      IOException, ValueTooSmallException {
7          Account account1 = new Account(1, "account1", 40);
8          Account account2 = new Account(2, "account2", 100);
9          FileOutputStream out = new FileOutputStream("acc.dat");
10         ObjectOutputStream outob = new ObjectOutputStream(out);
11         outob.writeObject(account1);
12         outob.writeObject(account2);
13         outob.close();
14         out.close();
15     }
16 }
```

In line 9, we create a FileOutputStream object, out, that outputs to file acc.dat. Line 10 creates an ObjectOutputStream object, outob, wrapped around out. It is important to note that an ObjectOutputStream object can be wrapped around any byte OutputStream, not just a FileOutputStream. In lines 11-12, we use the ObjectOutputStream writeObject method to write the account1 and account2 objects to outob.

ReadAccount is a program that reads the Account objects from the acc.dat file using an ObjectInputStream.

ReadAccount

```
1   import java.io.*;
2
3   class ReadAccount {
4
5       public static void main(String[] args) throws
6                       IOException, ClassNotFoundException {
7           FileInputStream in = new FileInputStream("acc.dat");
8           ObjectInputStream inobj = new ObjectInputStream(in);
9           Account acc1 = (Account) inobj.readObject();
10          Account acc2 = (Account) inobj.readObject();
11          System.out.println(" 1st number : " + acc1.accountNo);
12          System.out.println(" 2nd balance : " + acc2.balance);
13          inobj.close();
14          in.close();
15      }
16  }
```

ReadAccount

In lines 7-8, we create an ObjectInputStream object, inobj, wrapped around a FileInputStream object, in, which is connected to the acc.dat file. In lines 9-10, we use the ObjectInputStream readObject method to read the Account objects from the ObjectInputStream. readObject returns an Object type, so this needs to be cast to Account. readObject reads the objects in the same order as they were written to the acc.dat file. So acc1 corresponds to the account1 object in the WriteAccount program. readObject throws a ClassNotFoundException, so this exception should be present in the throws clause of the declaration (lines 5-6), together with the IOException thrown by all the stream methods.

The objects being written and read may be considerably more complex than this. For example, the Account class may have a reference to a Branch object. Furthermore, a number of Account objects may refer to the same Branch. To avoid making multiple copies of the Branch object, Java gives each object a serial number when writing to an ObjectOutputStream, hence the name **serialization** for this process. The process of reading back the object from the ObjectInputStream is called **deserialization**.

Note that when serializing an object, any referenced object must also be serializable. In fact, all objects in the referenced graph, known as **transitive closure**, must be serializable.

7.7.1 Controlling Serialization

Writing objects to a file that is possibly passed on to a third party before being read back in does mean a loss of control, which may cause concern for sensitive data. Of course, if we do not want an object to be serialized at all, we simply do not include the implements Serializable clause in the class declaration. If, however, we do not want individual member variables to be serialized, while allowing the serialization of others, we can use the **transient** keyword. For example, if we do not want to allow serialization of the account name, we change line 5 of Account to

```
transient String accountName;
```

If we now run WriteAccount, then ReadAccount, acc1.accountName and acc2.accountName will both be set to null. The effect would have been the same if accountName had been a static variable.

We may want to act defensively and guard against our file being corrupted. For example, recall that the Account class constructor will throw a ValueTooSmallException if an attempt is made to create an Account object with a negative balance. The readObject method (in lines 9–10 of ReadAccount) does not invoke the Account constructor. So if the acc.dat file became corrupted and the balance of account1 altered from 40.0 to −40.0, ReadAccount would still create an acc1 object with a balance of −40.0 violating our constructor constraint. To guard against this, we can add our own version of the readObject method to the Account class.

readObject

```
1  private void readObject(ObjectInputStream in) throws
2           IOException, ClassNotFoundException {
3      in.defaultReadObject();
4      if (balance < 0) {
5          throw new InvalidObjectException("Negative Balance");
6      }
7  }
```

readObject

The first statement must be a call of the ObjectInputStream defaultReadObject method (line 3), which reads the nonstatic, nontransient variables of the current class, Account, from the stream. defaultReadObject throws IOException and ClassNotFoundException, so these should be included in the throws clause of the declaration (lines 1–2). Any customized code follows the defaultReadObject call. In this case, we throw an InvalidObjectException if the balance is negative (lines 4–6). An InvalidObjectException is used to indicate that one or more deserialized objects have failed validation tests. As a defensive programming strategy, we would include all class constructor constraints in a readObject method if the class is being serialized.

In a similar manner, if we wish to customize the serialization process, we can add a writeObject method with customized code following a call to defaultWriteObject.

7.7.2 The jar Tool

At this point, we should mention the jar tool, provided as part of the Java SDK. The jar tool combines multiple files into a single jar archive file. jar files are compressed, like ZIP files, and can contain class files, serialized files, data files, images, and so on. This makes for convenient installation and distribution of files, and as we have seen in Chapter 5, we can include jar files in a classpath list. In the following example:

```
jar cvf  myjar Class1 Class2
```

cvf are jar options, indicating c, which creates a new or empty archive; v, which generates verbose output; and f, which specifies a jar file name, myjar in the example.

The jar tool automatically creates a manifest file, META-INF/MANIFEST.MF, which contains metadata describing the archive and is the first entry in the jar file. There are many options in the jar tool, for example, extracting files from an archive, listing contents of a jar file, and incorporating a customized manifest file.

chapter **8**

Developing GUIs

From its initial release, Java has included a number of classes for providing a graphical user interface (GUI). These classes were collectively known as the Abstract Window Toolkit (AWT). In Java versions 1.0 and 1.1, the AWT was the only means available for developing GUIs.

Java Swing classes for developing GUIs became available with the Sun Software Development Kit (SDK) platform 2; this included version 1.2 of the Java language, so 1.2 or a higher version of Java should be used to develop Swing programs. Swing provides a larger set of components than AWT and has a much richer functionality than the AWT equivalents. Furthermore, an AWT GUI takes on a look and feel dependent on the underlying operating system, whereas with Swing it is easy to specify a look and feel for most operating systems. In this chapter, we describe Swing. Swing, however, is a very large topic. There are many components with associated classes, methods, and interfaces. In this chapter, we can cover only the basics.

8.1   Introduction

Three basic concepts behind Swing are **containers**, **components**, and **event handling**. A container can be regarded as a screen or part of a screen. A container has an associated layout, which determines how components are arranged when they are added to a container. Atomic graphical user components, such as buttons, radio buttons, lists, and check boxes, are placed in containers. These can be top-level containers such as applets or frames, or can be placed in intermediate-level components such as panels, which in turn, are placed in the top-level containers. Event handling is the means by which user interactions are captured by a program, for example, a user makes a selection from a list of available items.

Swing has separate model and view classes for components. The data is held in a model class and is displayed in a view class. For example, the button data model interface is ButtonModel, and the supplied class that implements this interface is DefaultButtonModel. The button view class is JButton. For most components, the model is kept in the background, and the application program interacts with the view class through supplied methods. However, for more complex components, such as lists and tables, we need to explicitly interact with the model classes. One consequence of this separation of model and view classes is that it is possible for certain components to share models.

With the AWT, each component Java class had a corresponding device-dependent interface or peer that maps the classes execution code onto the underlying windowing system. So an AWT button includes Windows and Motif peer interfaces, for example. For this reason, AWT components are called heavyweight. Swing, on the other hand, is peerless, or lightweight, in that all component code is written entirely in Java. There are no device-dependent component peers; all the interaction with the underlying windowing system takes place within the top-level applet or frame containers. A consequence of this is that, whereas with AWT the GUI takes on a look and feel dependent on the underlying operating system, with Swing GUIs take on a Java look and feel by default although it is possible to specify a look and feel for most operating systems.

Although Swing supersedes the AWT, Swing still makes use of AWT classes especially in the area of event handling. Consequently, the Swing examples in this chapter will typically use java.awt as well as javax.Swing classes.

Figures 8.1 and 8.2 are examples of GUIs that we can create with Swing. These represent a simplified online equipment store. Figure 8.1 represents a screen where prospective customers enter their details. Figure 8.2 represents an order entry screen where customers place selected purchases in a shopping cart.

We refer to these screens throughout this chapter because they provide examples of a number of components and containers. In Section 8.9, we provide the program code behind Figure 8.1.

8.2 Swing Components

In this section, we describe a number of components available in the javax.swing.JComponent class. Figure 8.3 shows the inheritance hierarchy for both top-level containers and many of the lower-level components.

All the components within the JComponent class begin with a J. This distinguishes them from the earlier AWT components.

To abbreviate Swing class names, a program should include the statement

```
import javax.swing.*;
```

8.2.1 Button

This is one of the simplest components. The component labeled "Add to Cart," in Figure 8.2, is an example of a button. To create a button, first declare the button object to be of type JButton. For example,

```
JButton cartbutton;
```

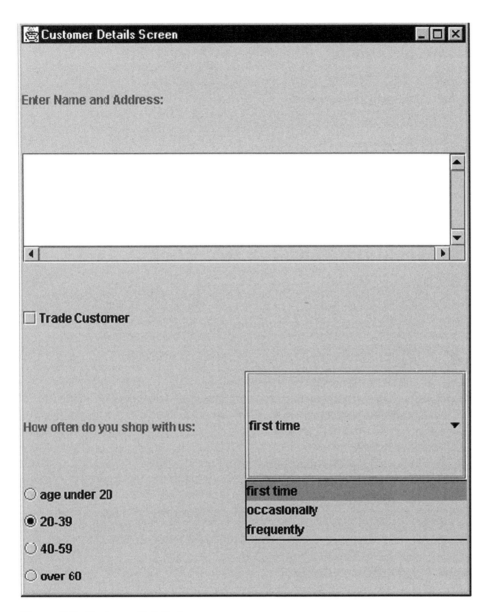

Figure 8.1: Customer Details Screen.

Then invoke the javax.swing.JButton constructor, as follows:

```
cartbutton = new JButton("Add to Cart");
```

This will create a button labeled with the supplied text. It is possible to create an unlabeled button using the constructor JButton(). All the layout examples in Section 8.5 also use buttons.

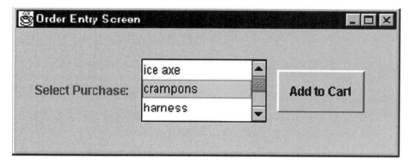

Figure 8.2: Order Entry Screen.

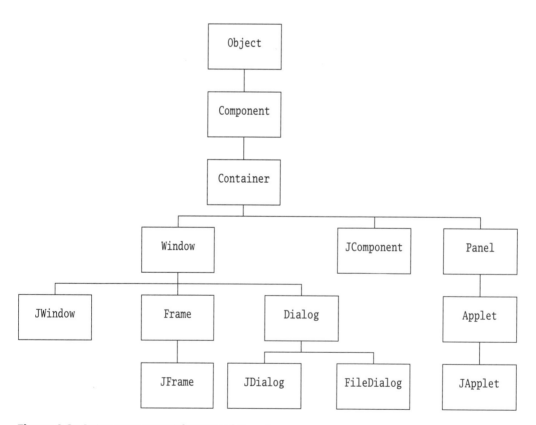

Figure 8.3: Swing component inheritance hierarchy.

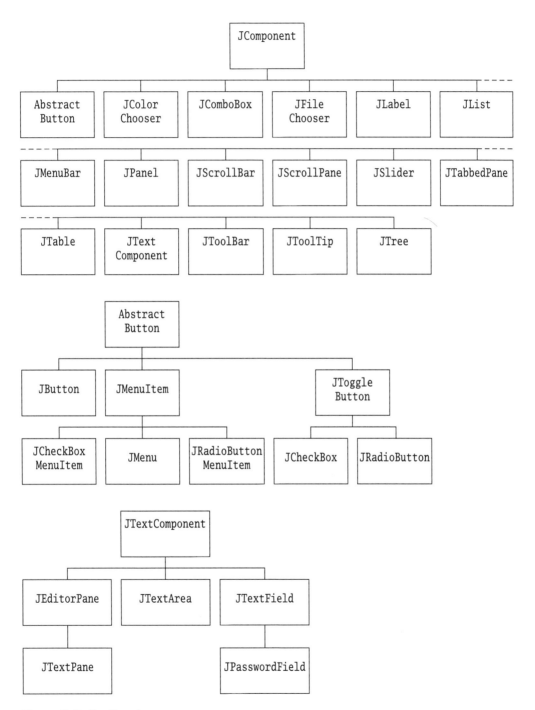

Figure 8.3: *Continued*

8.2.2   Combo Box

A combo box (or popup list) consists of a button that when clicked brings up a menu, and the user selects one item from this menu. This differs from a list in that before and after the menu selection is made only one item is visible. In Figure 8.1, the component dealing with shopping frequency labeled "first time," "occasionally," and "frequently" is an example of a combo box. To create a combo box, first declare the combo box object to be of type JComboBox. For example,

```
JComboBox freqButton;
```

Then invoke the javax.swing.JComboBox constructor, as follows:

```
freqButton = new JComboBox (comboString) ;
```

where comboString is a String array containing the combo box items

```
String[] comboString = {"first time", "occasionally",
                        "frequently"};
```

By default a combo box is uneditable. A combo box can be made editable by using the javax.swing.JComboBox.setEditable method, for example

```
freqButton.setEditable(true);
```

8.2.3   Check Box Button

A check box is a two-state button that can be clicked on or off. In Figure 8.1, the component labeled "Trade Customer" is an example of a check box button. To create a check box button, first declare the check box button object to be of type JCheckBox. For example,

```
JCheckBox tradeButton;
```

Next invoke the javax.swing.JCheckBox constructor, as follows:

```
tradeButton = new JCheckBox("Trade Customer", false);
```

This creates a check box button labeled "Trade Customer" with the initial state set to off. We could have used an alternative constructor JCheckBox("Trade Customer") because this sets the initial state to off by default. There is also the constructor JCheckBox(), which creates an unlabeled check box button with the initial state set to off.

8.2.4   Radio Button

A radio button group consists of a group of radio buttons with no more than one button selected at a time. In Figure 8.1, the buttons labeled "age under 20," "20-39," "40-59," "over 60" collectively form a radio button group. To create a radio button group, first declare the individual button objects to be of type JRadioButton. Then declare the radio button group object to be of type ButtonGroup. For example,

```
JRadioButton age1, age2, age3, age4;
ButtonGroup  ageButton;
```

Then invoke the javax.swing.ButtonGroup constructor, as follows:

```
ageButton = new ButtonGroup();
```

The individual buttons are created using the javax.swing.JRadioButton constructor, for example

```
age1 =  new JRadioButton("age under 20");
```

The individual buttons are then added to the radio button group using the javax.swing.Button-Group.add method, as follows:

```
ageButton.add(age1);
```

8.2.5 Text Field

A text field component is used for inputting or displaying a line of text information. To create a text field component, first declare the object to be of type JTextField. For example,

```
JTextField qtyfield;
```

Then invoke the javax.swing.JTextField constructor, for example

```
qtyfield = new JTextField (3);
```

where the constructor argument specifies the minimum number of columns in the text field itself. By default, a text field is editable; if a text field is to be used for outputting messages only, then use the javax.swing.text.JTextComponent method setEditable(false). Note that the JTextField class is a subclass of the JTextComponent class, as is the JTextArea class described in Section 8.2.6. Consequently, the setEditable method can also be used with text area components.

8.2.6 Text Area

The text area component is similar to the text field component, except in that it allows for multiple lines of text. In Figure 8.1, the component below the text "Enter Name and Address" is an example of a text area component. To create a text area component, first declare the object to be of type JTextArea. For example,

```
JTextArea addressArea;
```

By default, the text area is set up without scroll bars. To add scroll bars, you create a `JScrollPane` object then add the text area to the `JScrollPane` object. So declare a `JScrollPane` object, for example

```
JScrollPane addressPane;
```

Then invoke the `javax.swing.JTextArea` constructor, for example

```
addressArea = new JTextArea(3,12);
```

where the constructor arguments specify the minimum number of rows and columns in the text area itself. Now add `addressArea` to a scrollpane using the `JScrollPane` constructor, as follows:

```
addressPane = new JScrollPane(addressArea,
JScrollPane.VERTICAL_SCROLLBAR_ALWAYS,
JScrollPane.HORIZONTAL_SCROLLBAR_ALWAYS);
```

`JScrollPane.VERTICAL_SCROLLBAR_ALWAYS` and `JScrollPane.HORIZONTAL_SCROLLBAR_ALWAYS` indicate that the vertical and horizontal scrollbars are always visible. The default is to show no scrollbars until the text area becomes full with text entered by the user.

8.2.7 Label

A label component is used for displaying static text. In Figure 8.1, the text "How often do you shop with us:" is displayed using a label. To create a label, first declare the object to be of type `JLabel`. For example,

```
JLabel  freqLabel;
```

Then invoke the `javax.swing.JLabel` constructor, as follows:

```
freqLabel = new JLabel("How often do you shop with us: ");
```

8.2.8 List

A list component displays a scrolling list from which the user can select one or more items. A list differs from a combo box in that two or more items in the list can be made visible at all times. In Figure 8.2, the component to the right of the text "Select Purchase" is an example of a list. With Swing lists, we explicitly manipulate two models: the list and selection models. A list model is declared, list elements are added to this model, and the model is used when creating the list object. First declare a list model of type `DefaultListModel`. For example,

```
DefaultListModel shoppingListModel;
```

Then declare a list object to be of type `JList`. For example,

```
JList  shoppingList;
```

Then create the list model object using the `javax.swing.DefaultListModel` constructor, as follows:

```
shoppingListModel = new DefaultListModel();
```

Individual list elements are added to the model using the `javax.swing.DefaultList-Model.addElement` method. For example,

```
shoppingListModel.addElement("ice axe");
```

The list object itself is created using the `javax.swing.JList` constructor, as follows:

```
shoppingList = new JList(shoppingListModel);
```

Note the constructor requires the list model as an argument.

To specify that only one item can be selected from the list at any one time, use the `setSelectionMode` method. For example,

```
shoppingList.setSelectionMode(ListSelectionModel.SINGLE_SELECTION);
```

Other possible argument values are `SINGLE_INTERVAL_SELECTION`, which allows one contiguous interval to be selected, and `MULTIPLE_INTERVAL_SELECTION`, which allows multiple intervals to be selected. `MULTIPLE_INTERVAL_SELECTION` is the default. To set the number of list rows to be made visible, use the `javax.swing.JList.setVisibleRowCount` method. For example,

```
shoppingList.setVisibleRowCount(3);
```

will make three rows of `shoppingList` visible at any one time. Note that, like text areas, scrollbars are not automatically created for lists by Swing. To add scrollbars, create a scrollpane object, then add the list to the scrollpane object. For example,

```
JScrollPane sp = new JScrollPane(shoppingList);
```

8.3 Component Methods

There are a large number of methods in the `javax.swing.JComponent` class that deal with setting up borders, fonts, and colors, for example. Consequently, most of these methods are inherited by the components described in this chapter. In this section, we will describe just a few of these methods. For more details, consult the Sun API documentation.

8.3.1 Borders

To create borders around components, Java provides the `javax.swing.JComponent.setBorder` method. This method requires a border object as a parameter; the border object itself is provided by the `javax.swing.BorderFactory` class. There are many methods in this class; we will list just a few.

- `createLineBorder(color)` creates a line border with the specified color around the component. For example, the statement

    ```
    button1.setBorder(BorderFactory.createLineBorder(Color.red));
    ```

    creates a red line border around the `JButton` object `button1`. Note that to use the `Color.red` object, we would need the following statement in the application code:

    ```
    import java.awt.Color;
    ```

- `createLoweredBevelBorder()` and `createRaisedBevelBorder()` create borders with lowered and raised bevel edges. For example,

    ```
    label.setBorder(BorderFactory.createLoweredBevelBorder());
    ```

    creates a lowered bevel border for the `JLabel` object `label`.

8.3.2   Background and Foreground Colors

The `javax.swing.JComponent.setBackground` and `javax.swing.JComponent.setForeground` methods can be used to set background and foreground colors for a component. For example, the statements

```
cartbutton.setBackground(Color.black);
cartbutton.setForeground(Color.white);
```

set the background and foreground colors for the `JButton` object `cartbutton`.

8.3.3   Fonts

The `javax.swing.JComponent.setFont` method is used to set fonts for text associated with a component. This method requires a font object as a parameter; the font object itself is created by using the `java.awt.Font(font_name, font_style, font_size)` constructor. For example,

```
cartbutton.setFont(new Font("Italic", Font.ITALIC, 12));
```

sets the font associated with the `JButton` object `cartbutton` to 12 point italic. If `cartbutton` is a labeled button, then any text inside the button will use this font.

8.3.4   Enabling and Disabling Components

By default, all components are enabled. However, we may wish to disable a component. A disabled component cannot respond when clicked by the user. Having disabled a component, as a result of user actions we may wish to enable it again. Enabling and disabling are performed by the `javax.swing.JComponent.setEnabled(boolean)` method. For example, the statement

```
button2.setEnabled(false);
```

will disable the `JButton` object `button2`. Some disabled components, such as buttons, will take on a different (usually fainter) appearance from their enabled counterparts.

8.4 Swing Containers

8.4.1 Top-Level Containers

There are two types of top-level containers in Swing: **applets** and **windows**. An applet in Swing is a subclass of JApplet, as indicated by the declaration

```
public class Multiply extends JApplet
```

An applet will have an associated layout. An applet will contain components or other intermediate-level containers such as panels. An applet is downloaded by a Java-enabled Web browser then run: we discuss this aspect of applets in Section 8.10.

The second type of top-level container is a window. If we wish to add a GUI to a Java application, then we must use a window container. More precisely, we would use a subclass of a window, namely, a **frame**. A frame consists of a window together with a title bar. For example, Figure 8.1, being an application, uses a frame with the "Customer Details Screen" title bar. CustomerDetails in Section 8.9 provides the corresponding code. The application itself is a subclass of JFrame as indicated by the declaration

```
public class CustomerDetails extends JFrame .....
```

The javax.swing.JFrame class provides a number of methods: setTitle, setSize, and setVisible are among the most useful. setTitle is used to set the text in the title bar. setSize is used to set the size of the frame in pixels. The contents of a frame need to be made explicitly visible using the setVisible(true) method. A frame will have an associated layout. A frame will contain components or other intermediate-level containers such as panels.

Swing components can be added to panels, but panels and components cannot be directly added to top-level applet or frame containers. Top-level containers consist of an intermediate container, the **content pane**. The content pane contains all the visible components in the window's GUI. Components that would otherwise be added to the top-level container are added to the content pane. The methods javax.swing.JFrame.getContentPane and javax.swing.JApplet.getContentPane return the content pane for the current frame or applet, respectively. The content pane is actually an AWT (not Swing) object of type java.awt.Container, so to abbreviate class names a program should include the statement

```
import java.awt.Container;
```

The following is a code fragment for getting the content pane, cp, for the current applet or frame, and adding a button component, button1, to the content pane:

```
Container cp;
cp = this.getContentPane();
cp.add(button1);
```

8.4.2 Dialogues

Apart from frames, there is one other specialized window subclass, namely, Dialog. Dialogues typically provide messages within their own windows. The Swing Dialogue class,

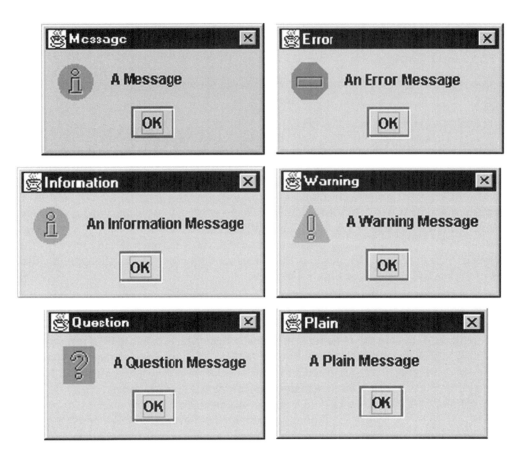

Figure 8.4: Standard dialogue windows.

javax.swing.JDialog is a subclass of java.awt.Dialog, which in turn, is a subclass of java.awt. Windows. This class is used to create a custom dialogue window. With Swing, a number of standard dialogue windows are available and easy to use. These standard dialogues are available through the javax.swing.JOptionPane class. Figure 8.4 shows the standard dialogue windows available with JOptionPane.

Dialogues usually have an associated parent frame. Typically, this frame will contain the application, and the dialogue will be created in response to the user performing a selection or some kind of action in the parent frame. Note that once a dialogue window appears, the user cannot perform any other action until the dialogue window has been clicked. The most useful method in the JOptionPane class is showMessageDialog. The statement

```
JOptionPane.showMessageDialog(fr, "A Message");
```

where fr is the parent frame, creates a default information message dialogue window with a corresponding information icon. The default title is "Message," and the message text is the second argument, namely, "A Message." The result is shown in Figure 8.4. Other invocations of the method are in the form

```
JOptionPane.showMessageDialog(fr, title, text, message_type);
```

where fr is the parent frame, title is the text to be displayed in the title portion of the window, text is the message displayed, and message_type determines the icon to be displayed. To illustrate this, the following statements produce the remaining dialogue windows shown in Figure 8.4:

```
JOptionPane.showMessageDialog(fr, "An Error Message",
    "Error", JOptionPane.ERROR_MESSAGE);

JOptionPane.showMessageDialog(fr, "An Information
  Message", "Information",
  JOptionPane.INFORMATION_MESSAGE);
```

Note that the preceding statement is similar to the first default dialogue, except in this case, the title text is supplied as a parameter.

```
JOptionPane.showMessageDialog(fr, "A Warning
  Message", "Warning", JOptionPane.WARNING_MESSAGE);

JOptionPane.showMessageDialog(fr, "A Question
  Message", "Question", JOptionPane.QUESTION_MESSAGE);

JOptionPane.showMessageDialog(fr, "A Plain Message",
    "Plain", JOptionPane.PLAIN_MESSAGE);
```

Note that for the preceding statement no icon is displayed.

We should briefly mention here a few other classes that provide for specialized dialogues similar to JOptionPane. The javax.swing.ProgressMonitor class is used to show the progress of an operation. This is done by means of a dialogue window and progress bar. The javax.swing.JColorChooser class is used to manipulate and select a color. The javax.swing.JFileChooser class is used to choose a file. Consult the Sun API documentation for details.

8.4.3 Intermediate-Level Containers

Intermediate-level containers contain Swing components, but themselves will be contained within one of the two top-level containers, applet or frame.

Panel

A panel is a grouping of Swing components. A GUI screen consists of any number of panels. Like all containers, a panel will have a layout type associated with it, this determines how the components within a panel are displayed. Panels differ from other containers in that a panel itself can contain subpanels as well as components.

The declaration

```
JPanel mypanel;
```

declares a mypanel object of type JPanel. The statement

```
mypanel = new JPanel();
```

creates the mypanel object using the JPanel() class constructor.

Scrollpane

Scrollpanes can be used to provide a scrollable view for any component whose size can change dynamically. Candidate components are text areas and lists, for example. A scrollpane will include horizontal and vertical scrollbars.

There are a number of constructors in the javax.swing.JScrollPane class. The simplest is JScrollPane(component). This will show scrollbars only if the contents of the component are larger than the scrollable view. So in a text area component, for example, scrollbars will be shown only when the user has filled the viewable text area with text. Another form of the constructor is JScrollPane(component, vertical_policy, horizontal_policy). vertical_policy and horizontal_policy specify the behavior of the vertical and horizontal scrollbars, respectively. vertical_policy takes one of the following values:

- JScrollPane.VERTICAL_SCROLLBAR_AS_NEEDED. This specifies that vertical scrollbars are shown only when needed.

- JScrollPane.VERTICAL_SCROLLBAR_ALWAYS. This specifies that vertical scrollbars are always shown.

- JScrollPane.VERTICAL_SCROLLBAR_NEVER. This specifies that vertical scrollbars are never shown.

horizontal_policy takes on similar values regarding horizontal scrollbar behavior. Once a scrollpane object is created, it is added to the content pane. We have seen examples of scrollpanes with text areas and lists in Sections 8.2.6 and 8.2.8, respectively.

8.5 Layouts

All containers, both top-level and intermediate, have an associated layout. Swing provides the following layouts: FlowLayout, BorderLayout, GridLayout, GridbagLayout, CardLayout, and BoxLayout. We describe FlowLayout, BorderLayout, and GridLayout in the following sections. Consult the Sun API documentation for details of remaining layouts.

8.5.1 FlowLayout

This is the simplest type of layout. Components are added to a container from left to right. If no horizontal space is available for a component, a new row is started. Figure 8.5 is an example of a frame container using FlowLayout (the components are actually buttons, but they can be

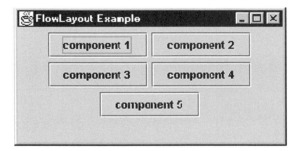

Figure 8.5: FlowLayout.

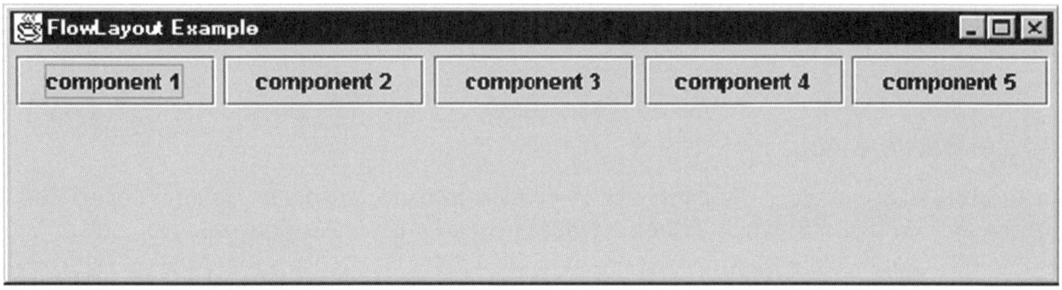

Figure 8.6: Dynamically adjusted FlowLayout.

any Swing component). If the window is dynamically widened by dragging with a mouse, all the components will in due course fit on one row, resulting in Figure 8.6.

FlowLayout is the default layout type for all JPanel objects. Note that there is a default horizontal and vertical gap of 5 pixels between the components. By default, each row of components is center justified. The FlowLayout is an AWT feature, so to abbreviate class names, programs should include the statement

```
import java.awt.FlowLayout;
```

To create a FlowLayout container with these defaults, use the following statements:

```
cp = this.getContentPane();
cp.setLayout(new FlowLayout());
```

where cp is the current applet or frame content pane. getContentPane and setLayout are methods in both javax.swing.JApplet and javax.swing.JFrame classes.

To specify an alignment, use the constructor FlowLayout(align), where align is either FlowLayout.LEFT (left justified), FlowLayout.RIGHT (right justified) or FlowLayout.CENTER (center justified, the default). To specify an alignment and component gap sizes, use the constructor FlowLayout(align, horizgap, vertgap), where horizgap is the horizontal gap and vertgap is the vertical gap in pixels.

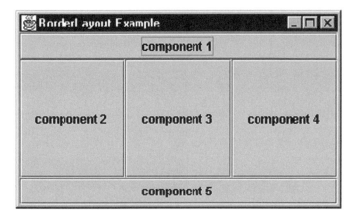

Figure 8.7: BorderLayout.

8.5.2   BorderLayout

In the BorderLayout type, the container is divided into five sections, namely, north, west, center, east, and south. When adding a component to a BorderLayout container, one of the above five sections is specified. BorderLayout is the default layout for content panes. Figure 8.7 is an example of a BorderLayout on a frame consisting of five components (again actually buttons).

BorderLayout is an AWT feature, so to abbreviate class names, programs must include the statement

```
import java.awt.BorderLayout;
```

To create a BorderLayout container, use the following statements:

```
cp = this.getContentPane();
cp.setLayout(new BorderLayout());
```

where cp is the current applet or frame content pane. This creates no gaps between the components. If gaps are desired, use the constructor BorderLayout(horizgap, vertgap), the gaps being specified in pixels. A component is added to a BorderLayout container with a statement of the form add(component, BorderLayout.SECTION). The following code illustrates this for Figure 8.7:

```
cp = this.getContentPane();
cp.setLayout(new BorderLayout());
/* set up buttons and add them to content pane */
button1 = new JButton("component 1");
cp.add(button1, BorderLayout.NORTH);
button2 = new JButton("component 2");
cp.add(button2, BorderLayout.WEST);
```

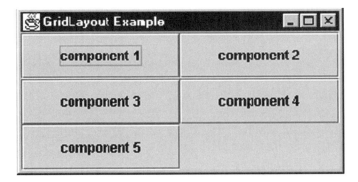

Figure 8.8: GridLayout.

```
button3 = new JButton("component 3");
cp.add(button3, BorderLayout.CENTER);
button4 = new JButton("component 4");
cp.add(button4, BorderLayout.EAST);
button5 = new JButton("component 5");
cp.add(button5, BorderLayout.SOUTH);
```

8.5.3 GridLayout

In a GridLayout container, components are placed in a grid of cells. The statement

```
cp.setLayout(new GridLayout(r, c));
```

specifies a GridLayout with r rows and c columns for the content pane cp. By default, there are no gaps between components. Again, if gaps are desired, use the constructor GridLayout(r, c, horizgap, vertgap).

Figure 8.8 illustrates a GridLayout frame with a grid of three rows and two columns. The GridLayout is an AWT feature, so to abbreviate class names, programs must include the statement

```
import java.awt.GridLayout;
```

8.6 Specifying Look and Feel

Recall that Swing graphical user interfaces (GUIs) take on a Java look and feel by default. All the figures in this chapter have used the Swing Java look and feel. However, it is possible to specify a windowing system look and feel.

Look and feel is set by the javax.swing.UIManager.setLookAndFeel method. This method has one parameter, the name of the class that determines look and feel. These classes are not part of the Java language itself, but rather classes within a package (com.sun.java.swing) supplied by the Java Software Development Kit (SDK). The classes are as follows:

- com.sun.java.swing.plaf.windows.WindowsLookAndFeel for Windows (32 bit only) operating systems

- com.sun.java.swing.plaf.motif.MotifLookAndFeel for CDE/Motif look and feel on Sun platforms

The setLookAndFeel method must be invoked within a try catch block. For example, the following code fragment will create a Windows look and feel:

```
try {
    UIManager.setLookAndFeel(
    "com.sun.java.swing.plaf.windows.WindowsLookAndFeel");
} catch (Exception e) { }
```

8.7   Event Handling

All of our examples have been write only: displaying GUI objects on a window or panel, but with no means of the user communicating back to the program. This communication is provided by the Swing event-handling mechanism.

The basic idea of event handling is to register an object to act as a listener for a particular type of event on a particular component. Typically, the listener object will be the applet or application instance. An event, such as clicking on a component, causes an event object to be sent to all registered listeners. The class corresponding to the listener object will contain methods from the listener interface that handle the event.

The listener interface that is used depends on the type of event the application wishes to capture. For example, the event of a user clicking on a button would be handled by the ActionListener, a keystroke by the KeyListener, a mouse movement by the MouseListener interfaces, and so on. Interfaces were covered in Section 5.4. Recall that all the methods declared in an interface must have their method bodies written in the application program. For ActionListener, there is only one corresponding method, actionPerformed, so this method would perform any actions resulting from the event. On the other hand, the KeyListener interface has three corresponding methods: keyPressed, keyReleased, and keyTyped, so all these would need to be present in the application code.

To abbreviate event-handling class names, the application should include the statement

```
import java.awt.event.*;
```

The class declaration must list any listeners that the class implements. For example, suppose we have a class, CustomerDetails, which is a frame that implements ActionListener and ItemListener. The class declaration would then be

```
public class CustomerDetails extends JFrame
            implements ActionListener, ItemListener {
```

The next step is to register the class instance to act as a listener for one or more specific components. For example, the following statement registers the CustomerDetails object to act as an ActionListener for the tradeButton button:

```
tradeButton.addItemListener(this);
```

The argument, this, indicates the object corresponding to the current class, namely, CustomerDetails. Each button object for which we wish to handle a corresponding event will have a corresponding listener registration statement. Each listener interface has a corresponding "add" method for registering a listener object.

The final step is to write the listener method bodies themselves. The ActionListener interface has one corresponding method, actionPerformed. ItemListener also has just one corresponding method, itemStateChanged.

These two methods are described in detail in Sections 8.7.1 and 8.7.2. At this stage, you should note that a number of events can invoke the same listener. For example, a user clicking on a button or pressing return after entering text in a text field can generate an ActionListener event in both cases. Consequently, the code in actionPerformed needs to distinguish between button and text field events. Even if only one component type, button, say, is present in a frame or applet, the code would need to distinguish between the different button components.

In the following sections, we describe a few of the most common listener interfaces. A full list of listener interfaces, their associated methods and the components that invoke the listener, is given in Appendix B. Details of all the listener interfaces can be found in the Sun API documentation.

8.7.1 ActionListener

ActionListeners are used to respond to action events. Action events are typically created by clicking a button or pressing return in a text field. The ActionListener interface consists of a single method, actionPerformed. Specifically, this method has the signature

```
void actionPerformed(ActionEvent e);
```

where e is an object of type ActionEvent. The java.awt.event.ActionEvent class contains a number of methods; two of the most useful are getSource and getActionCommand. getSource returns the object that generated the event. getActionCommand returns the command string associated with the component that generated the event. By default, this string is the text associated with a labeled component; you can explicitly set the command string using the setActionCommand method.

As an example, suppose we have registered action listeners for a combo box, freqButton, and a radio button group, age, consisting of individual radio buttons age1, age2, age3, and age4. These could represent the shopping frequency combo box and age radio button in the Customer Details screen of Figure 8.1. The actionPerformed method is shown next.

actionPerformed

```
1    public void actionPerformed(ActionEvent e) {
2        if (e.getSource() instanceof JComboBox) {
3            System.out.println("Customer shops : " +
4            freqButton.getSelectedItem() );
5        } else if (e.getSource() instanceof JRadioButton) {
6            if (age1.isSelected() ) {
7                System.out.println("Customer is under 20");
8            } else if (age2.isSelected() ) {
9                System.out.println("Customer is 20 - 39");
10           } else if (age3.isSelected() ) {
11               System.out.println("Customer is 40 - 59");
12           } else if (age4.isSelected() ) {
13               System.out.println("Customer is over 60");
14           }
15       }
16   }
```

actionPerformed

If the user clicks the freqButton combo box, a message is printed to the console informing us how frequently the customer shops. Since we have also registered an action listener for the age radio button, the statement (line 2)

```
if (e.getSource() instanceof JComboBox) {
```

determines whether the event corresponds to the clicking of a combo box. Since the application is registered to listen to only one combo box, freqButton, we can use the javax.swing.JComboBox.getSelectedItem method to determine the currently selected item.

In line 5, we check if the event corresponds to the user clicking a radio button. In line 6, we use the javax.swing.JCheckBox.isSelected method to determine if the age1 radio button has been selected. The isSelected method returns true if the radio button is currently selected, otherwise false. We perform similar tests for the remaining radio buttons forming the radio button group.

8.7.2   ItemListener

ItemListeners are used to respond to item events. These are generated whenever an item's state changes. Typically, this occurs when an item is selected or deselected from a check box or a radio button. If, for example, a particular radio button is currently selected and another radio button is clicked, the item event is fired twice: once when the current radio button is deselected, and a second time when the new radio button is selected. The ItemListener interface consists of a single method, itemStateChanged. Specifically, this method has the signature

```
        void itemStateChanged(ItemEvent e);
```

where e is an object of type ItemEvent. The java.awt.event.ItemEvent class contains a number of methods, including getSource. As with an action event, getSource returns the object that generated the event.

As an example, suppose we have registered an item listener for a check box, tradeButton. This could represent the Trade Customer check box in Figure 8.1. The itemStateChanged method is shown next.

itemStateChanged

```
1   public void itemStateChanged (ItemEvent e) {
2          if (e.getSource() instanceof JCheckBox) {
3              JCheckBox buttonLabel = (JCheckBox)
4                                    e.getItemSelectable();
5              if (buttonLabel == tradeButton){
6                  if (e.getStateChange() == e.SELECTED) {
7                      System.out.println("Customer is trade");
8                  } else {
9                      System.out.println("Customer is not trade");
10                 }
11             }
12         }
13     }
```

itemStateChanged

The statement (line 2)

```
        if (e.getSource() instanceof JCheckBox) {
```

determines whether the event source is a check box. In that case, in lines 3-4, we use the java.awt.event.ItemEvent.getItemSelectable method to obtain the originator of the item event. This is then cast to a JCheckBox, buttonLabel. We can then use the ItemEvent.getState-Change method to determine whether tradeButton has been checked.

8.7.3 ListSelectionListener

The ListSelectionListener interface is used to handle list selection events. These occur whenever the selection in a list or table has changed. Note that since the ListSelectionListener is a Swing and not an AWT listener interface, to abbreviate class names, the program should include the following statement:

```
        import javax.swing.event.*;
```

The ListSelectionListener interface consists of a single method, valueChanged(ListSelection-Event e), where e is an object of type ListSelectionEvent. The method javax.swing.event.ListSelectionEvent.getSource obtains the source object generating the event. The value-Changed example uses the javax.swing.JList.getSelectedValue to determine the list item that has been selected.

valueChanged

```
1  public void valueChanged(ListSelectionEvent e) {
2      if (e.getSource() instanceof JList) {
3          if (shoppingList.getSelectedValue().equals("ice axe")) {
4              System.out.println("ice axe selected");
5          }
6      }
7  }
```

8.7.4   Adapters in Event Handling

All the listener interfaces we have described so far have just one associated method. Many other interfaces have several associated methods. We will use one such interface, WindowListener, as an example throughout this section. WindowListener has windowActivated, windowClosed, windowClosing, windowDeactivated, windowDeiconified, windowIconified, and windowOpened as associated methods. Recall from Section 5.4 that a class implementing an interface must have bodies for all the interface methods. This means that if we are interested in setting up only one listener interface method, windowClosing, say, we would need to write empty bodies for the other methods along the lines of

```
public void windowActivated((WindowEvent e)) { }
```

To avoid this, we can use an **adapter** class: this implements empty bodies for all the interface methods. All event listener interfaces containing more than one method definition have a corresponding adapter class. In the case of WindowListener, this is WindowAdapter. The application class is defined as a subclass of the adapter class, and any nonempty interface methods are written within the application class.

If our application is a frame or applet subclass, then we cannot also define the application as a subclass of WindowAdapter. However, we can use inner classes. The following code fragment shows an inner class, MyWindowAdapter, that implements the windowClosing method. This, in turn, terminates the application when the user closes the main window.

```
class MyWindowAdapter extends WindowAdapter {
    public void windowClosing(WindowEvent e) {
```

```
            System.exit(0);
        }
    }
```

The listener registration is performed by the statement

```
    this.addWindowListener(new MyWindowAdapter() );
```

Note we do not register the application object to act as a listener, but an instance of the MyWindowAdapter class. The component for which we are registering a listener is the component involved when a user shuts the main window. This component is the current frame instance, identified by the keyword this.

If we create only a single object of the MyWindowAdapter class, we can dispense with giving the adapter subclass a name by using an **anonymous inner class**. We can replace the preceding MyWindowAdapter class and the addWindowListener statement with

```
    this.addWindowListener(new WindowAdapter() {
        public void windowClosing(WindowEvent e) {
            System.exit(0);
        }
    });
```

This syntax reads as define an anonymous inner class as a subclass of WindowAdapter, create an instance of this inner class, and use this instance as an argument to the addWindowListener method.

8.8 Painting with Swing

With Swing, we do not draw text or images directly onto a frame or applet. A component subclass is created, usually a subclass of JPanel, and the painting is performed in the subclasses' paintComponent method. An instance of this component subclass is then created and added to the content pane. The PaintPanel example shows a panel subclass performing painting.

PaintPanel

```
1  import javax.swing.*;
2  import java.awt.Dimension;
3  import java.awt.Graphics;
4
5  class PaintPanel extends JPanel {
6      public PaintPanel() {
7          setPreferredSize(new Dimension(110, 24));
8      }
9
```

```
10      public void paintComponent (Graphics g) {
11          super.paintComponent(g);
12          g.drawString("Text to be drawn" , 20, getHeight()  );
13      }
14  }
```

The constructor, PaintPanel, uses the javax.swing.JPanel.setPreferredSize method to set the size of the panel, in this case, 110 pixels wide and 24 pixels high. The first statement in the paintComponent method must be

```
super.paintComponent(g);
```

This causes the component to paint its background. The java.awt.Graphics.drawString method is used to paint the text. Two useful methods in javax.swing.JComponent that can be used with drawString are getHeight and getWidth. These return the current component height and width, respectively.

An instance of PaintPanel is created and then added to the content pane, cp, as follows:

```
PaintPanel p = new PaintPanel();
cp.add(p);
```

8.9   CustomerDetails Example

In this section, we bring together topics discussed in this chapter by walking through the CustomerDetails code that produces Figure 8.1.

CustomerDetails

```
1   import javax.swing.*;
2   import java.awt.Dimension;
3   import java.awt.GridLayout;
4   import java.awt.event.*;
5   import java.awt.Color;
6   import java.awt.Container;
7
8   public class CustomerDetails extends JFrame
9                implements ActionListener, ItemListener {
10      JTextArea    addressArea;
11      JScrollPane  addressPane;
12      JLabel       addressLabel;
13      JLabel       freqLabel;
```

```
14      JComboBox    freqButton;
15      JCheckBox    tradeButton;
16      JRadioButton age1;
17      JRadioButton age2;
18      JRadioButton age3;
19      JRadioButton age4;
20      ButtonGroup  ageButton;
21      JPanel       agePanel;
22      JPanel       freqPanel;
23      Container    cp;
24      String[]     comboString= {"first time",
25                                 "occasionally", "frequently"};
26
27          public CustomerDetails() {
28
29          /* set up layout panels */
30          cp = this.getContentPane();
31          cp.setLayout(new GridLayout(5,1));
32          agePanel = new JPanel();
33          agePanel.setLayout(new GridLayout(4,1) );
34          freqPanel = new JPanel();
35          freqPanel.setLayout(new GridLayout(1,2) );
36
37          /* set up name address label */
38          addressLabel = new JLabel("Enter Name and Address:");
39          cp.add(addressLabel) ;
40
41          /* set up name address text area */
42          addressArea = new JTextArea(3,12);
43          addressPane = new JScrollPane(addressArea,
44          JScrollPane.VERTICAL_SCROLLBAR_ALWAYS,
45          JScrollPane.HORIZONTAL_SCROLLBAR_ALWAYS);
46          cp.add(addressPane);
47
48          /* set up Trade Customer Checkbox button */
49          tradeButton = new JCheckBox("Trade Customer", false);
50          tradeButton.addItemListener(this);
51          cp.add(tradeButton);
52
53          /* set up shopping frequency combo box  */
54          freqLabel = new JLabel(
55                  "How often do you shop with us: ");
56          freqPanel.add(freqLabel);
57          freqButton = new JComboBox(comboString);
58          freqButton.addActionListener(this);
59          freqPanel.add(freqButton);
60          cp.add(freqPanel);
```

```
61
62          /* set up age range radio button */
63          ageButton = new ButtonGroup();
64          age1 =  new JRadioButton("age under 20");
65          age2 =  new JRadioButton("20-39");
66          age3 =  new JRadioButton("40-59");
67          age4 =  new JRadioButton("over 60");
68          ageButton.add(age1);
69          ageButton.add(age2);
70          ageButton.add(age3);
71          ageButton.add(age4);
72          age1.addActionListener(this);
73          age2.addActionListener(this);
74          age3.addActionListener(this);
75          age4.addActionListener(this);
76          agePanel.add(age1);
77          agePanel.add(age2);
78          agePanel.add(age3);
79          agePanel.add(age4);
80          cp.add(agePanel);
81          this.addWindowListener(new WindowAdapter() {
82              public void windowClosing(WindowEvent e) {
83                  System.exit(0);
84              }
85          });
86      }
87
88      // actionPerformed is ActionListener interface method
89      // which responds to action event of selecting
90      // combo box or radio button
91      public void actionPerformed(ActionEvent e) {
92          if (e.getSource() instanceof JComboBox) {
93              System.out.println("Customer shops: " +
94              freqButton.getSelectedItem() );
95          } else if (e.getSource() instanceof JRadioButton) {
96              if (age1.isSelected() ) {
97                  System.out.println("Customer is under 20");
98              } else if (age2.isSelected() ) {
99                  System.out.println("Customer is 20 - 39");
100             } else if (age3.isSelected() ) {
101                 System.out.println("Customer is 40 - 59");
102             } else if (age4.isSelected() ) {
103                 System.out.println("Customer is over 60");
104             }
105         }
106     }
107
```

```
108     // itemStateChanged is ItemListener interface method
109     // which responds to item event of clicking checkbox
110     public void itemStateChanged (ItemEvent e) {
111         if (e.getSource() instanceof JCheckBox) {
112             JCheckBox buttonLabel = (JCheckBox)
113                                 e.getItemSelectable();
114         if (buttonLabel == tradeButton){
115             if (e.getStateChange() == e.SELECTED) {
116                 System.out.println("Customer is trade");
117             } else {
118                 System.out.println("Customer is not trade");
119             }
120         }
121     }
122     }

124     // main method creates CustomerDetails frame
125     public static void main(String args[]) {
126         CustomerDetails cd = new CustomerDetails ();
127         cd.setTitle("Customer Details Screen");
128         cd.setSize(400,600);
129         cd.setVisible(true);
130     }
131 }
```

CustomerDetails

The class declaration (lines 8-9) indicates that this is a frame that implements the ActionListener and ItemListener interfaces. Lines 30-31 specify that the frame's content pane has an associated GridLayout of five rows and one column. The GridLayout schema consists of the following components and panels:

addressLabel	JLabel Component
addressArea	JTextArea Component
tradeButton	JCheckbox Component
freqPanel	JPanel
agePanel	JPanel

We have used this schema to ensure that the screen is equally divided among the five components or panels.

The freqPanel panel itself uses a GridLayout of one row and two columns, and consists of the following components:

freqLabel	JLabel Component	freqButton	JComboBox Component

The agePanel panel itself uses a GridLayout of four rows and one column, and consists of the following components:

age1   JRadioButton Component
age2   JRadioButton Component
age3   JRadioButton Component
age4   JRadioButton Component

These components make up the ageButton ButtonGroup. The code creates the preceding components and panels, then adds them to their assigned panels or directly to the content pane.

Note that having created a JTextArea component, addressArea, we do not add the component directly to the content pane but first to a scroll pane. The statement (lines 43–45)

```
addressPane = new JScrollPane(addressArea,
JScrollPane.VERTICAL_SCROLLBAR_ALWAYS,
JScrollPane.HORIZONTAL_SCROLLBAR_ALWAYS);
```

creates a scrollpane object, addressPane, with horizontal and vertical scrollbars always visible. In line 46, addressPane is added to the content pane.

In line 49, note that when creating the tradeButton check box, by setting the second argument of the constructor to false, the check box is initially set unchecked.

In line 50, we register this frame to act as an ItemListener for the tradeButton component, and (line 58) as an ActionListener for the freqButton component.

In line 63, the ageButton radio button group object is created using the ButtonGroup constructor. Individual radio buttons are then assigned to the radio button group using the JRadioButton constructor. For example, in line 64,

```
age1 =  new JRadioButton("age under 20");
```

This sets the radio button to unchecked by default. If we want to initially display a radio button as checked, we would use the JRadioButton(text, boolean) constructor, as follows:

```
age1 =  new JRadioButton("age under 20", true);
```

We use the javax.swing.ButtonGroup.add method to add the radio button to the group. For example, in line 68,

```
ageButton.add(age1);
```

Note that we register this frame to act as an ActionListener for each individual radio button (lines 72–75).

In lines 81–85, we add an anonymous inner class to terminate the application when the user closes the main window, as described in Section 8.7.4.

The actionPerformed and itemStateChanged methods were described in Sections 8.7.1 and 8.7.2, respectively.

In the main method (lines 125–130), the statement (line 126)

```
CustomerDetails cd = new CustomerDetails ();
```

creates an instance, cd, of the frame CustomerDetails. We then set the frame's title and size, and make the frame visible.

8.10   Applets

In this section, we describe a simple applet, MultiplyApplet.java. This applet performs the same function as the Multiply application in Chapter 1, namely, to output the product of two integers supplied as parameters. In contrast to an application that is a standalone program, an applet is invoked by a Web browser from a Web page. A Web page written in HTML (hypertext markup language) will contain an applet tag that specifies the location of the applet class files and the position of the applet on the Web page. The browser retrieves the applet class files across the Internet (of course, the applet class files may reside in the user's local computer), and runs the applet using the browser's JVM. Multiply.html is an example of a minimal Web page that loads MultiplyApplet.

Multiply.html

```
 1   <HTML>
 2   <HEAD>
 3   <TITLE>
 4   HTML Page which loads Multiply Applet
 5   </TITLE>
 6   </HEAD>
 7   <APPLET CODE = "MultiplyApplet"  WIDTH = 250 HEIGHT =
 8   200  NAME = "MultiplyApplet" >
 9   <PARAM NAME = "firstInt" VALUE = "7">
10   <PARAM NAME = "secondInt" VALUE = "12">
11   </APPLET>
12   </HTML>
```

Multiply.html

We do not cover HTML in this book; furthermore, it is not necessary to have a knowledge of HTML to understand applets. It is sufficient to note that an HTML page consists of a series of tags and content that describe how a Web page looks when displayed. Tags start with a < character and end with a > character. Some tags have a slash after the leading <. The tag without the slash is the start tag, and the tag with the slash is the end tag. Tags can be nested within one another.

An HTML applet tag takes the form <APPLET>...</APPLET>. Within the tag are applet details such as the width and height of the applet display area. In particular, the clause in line 7,

```
CODE = "MultiplyApplet"
```

gives the name of the applet class file.

```
WIDTH = 250
```

gives the initial width of the applet display area in pixels.

```
HEIGHT = 200
```

gives the initial height of the applet display area in pixels. In line 8,

```
NAME = "MultiplyApplet"
```

is the name given to the applet instance. This makes it possible for applets on the same page to communicate with each other. In line 9,

```
<PARAM NAME = "firstInt" VALUE = "7">
```

assigns the value 7 to the named parameter, firstInt. The applet itself, MultiplyApplet, then uses the parameter names, in this case, firstInt and secondInt, to retrieve the parameters set in the HTML page, as we shall see shortly.

We now turn to the MultiplyApplet.java code itself.

MultiplyApplet.java

```
 1   public class MultiplyApplet extends java.applet.Applet {
 2
 3       private String param1;
 4       private String param2;
 5       private String resultString;
 6       private int arg1;
 7       private int arg2;
 8       private int result;
 9
10       public void init() {
11           param1 = getParameter("firstInt");
12           param2 = getParameter("secondInt");
13           arg1 = Integer.parseInt(param1);
14           arg2 = Integer.parseInt(param2);
15           result = arg1 * arg2;
16       }
17
18       public void paint(java.awt.Graphics g) {
19           resultString = Integer.toString(result);
```

```
20          g.drawString("The product of " + param1 + " and " +
21          param2 + " is " + resultString, 50, 100);
22      }
23  }
```

MultiplyApplet.java

Note that just like a Java application, Java applet source code is stored in a file with a name of the form className.java. The declaration (line 1),

```
public class MultiplyApplet extends java.applet.Applet {
```

indicates that the MultiplyApplet class is an applet. More accurately, MultiplyApplet is a subclass of the java.applet.Applet class. As such, MultiplyApplet inherits a number of methods from the Applet class.

Note that we do not have a main method. main methods are the starting points for standalone applications written in Java. The life cycle of an applet is different. An applet usually contains an init method; this method is invoked when the applet is loaded into a Web browser for the first time. Typically, init will perform initialization; in our simple example, init actually performs the multiplication of the two input parameters.

getparameter is an Applet method that returns the value of the named parameter. The named parameter must be present in the PARAM NAME tag in the HTML Web page. For example, in the statement (line 11)

```
param1 = getParameter("firstInt");
```

the named parameter "firstInt" corresponds to that in line 9,

```
<PARAM NAME = "firstInt" VALUE = "7">
```

of the HTML page, Multiply.html.

In line 18 of MultiplyApplet.java, the paint method is used to output to the applet drawing area. It overrides the paint method of the java.awt.Component class. The paint method takes an object g of type java.awt.Graphics as an argument. This object represents the applet drawing area. drawString is one of the methods in the Graphics class, and lines 20–21 draw the text corresponding to the supplied String to the applet drawing area, g, at x and y coordinates of 50 and 100.

As with applications, we use the javac compiler to produce a bytecode file Multiply-Applet.class.

One way to test an applet is to use Sun's Applet Viewer, which can be downloaded from their Web site as part of the Java SDK. Assuming that the Applet Viewer, Multiply.html

Figure 8.9: Applet Viewer invoking MultiplyApplet.

file, and `MultiplyApplet.class` files all reside in the same directory, we can issue the command

> `appletviewer Multiply.html`

The result is shown in Figure 8.9.

Assuming we have a Java-enabled Web browser installed on our test computer, we simply need to enter the full HTML file path name in the browser's address area. For example, Figure 8.10 shows the output from a Microsoft Internet Explorer version 5 Web browser when the path name `C:\JavaExamples\Multiply.html` has been entered in the address area.

8.10.1 Swing Applets

The applet described in the previous section was a subclass of `java.applet.Applet` and as such did not use any Swing features. The advantage of this is that the applet can be invoked by any Java 1.0-enabled Web browser (virtually all browsers). The disadvantage is that we are restricted to the limited AWT graphical user interface. Applets can use the Swing features described earlier in this chapter. However, most browsers such as Microsoft Internet Explorer or Netscape Navigator that support only Java version 1.1 can run version 1.2 or Swing applets if they install a Java 1.2 plugin. However, if we use a plugin, we cannot use the <APPLET> tag in an HTML page. The tags that are used are more complex and differ from browser to browser; however, Sun does provide a utility for converting an <APPLET> tag to the plugin equivalent. The next listing shows the Swing version of the `MultiplyApplet` example described in the previous section.

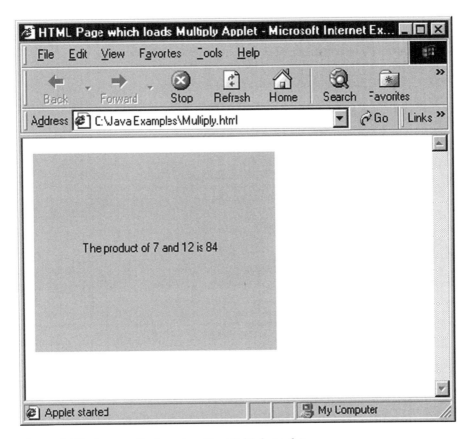

Figure 8.10: Internet Explorer invoking MultiplyApplet.

MultiplyApplet—Swing version

```
1   import javax.swing.*;
2   import java.awt.Container;
3
4   public class MultiplyApplet extends JApplet {
5       private String param1;
6       private String param2;
7       private String resultString;
8       private int arg1;
9       private int arg2;
10      private int result;
11      Container cp;
12
13      public void init() {
```

```
14              param1 = getParameter("firstInt");
15              param2 = getParameter("secondInt");
16              arg1 = Integer.parseInt(param1);
17              arg2 = Integer.parseInt(param2);
18              result = arg1 * arg2;
19              cp = getContentPane();
20              Panel p = new Panel ();
21              cp.add(p);
22          }
23
24      class Panel extends JPanel {
25
26          public void paintComponent (java.awt.Graphics g) {
27              super.paintComponent(g);
28              resultString = Integer.toString(result);
29              g.drawString("The product of " + param1 + " and " +
30              param2 + " is " + resultString, 50, 100);
31          }
32      }
33  }
```

MultiplyApplet—Swing version

There are only a couple of differences between the Swing and AWT versions. The first point to note is that our Multiply applet is a subclass of JApplet and not Applet. The JApplet class is actually a subclass of Applet and consequently inherits many of its methods. The second difference is that we do not draw the result directly on to the applet but create a JPanel subclass, Panel, and use the subclass paintComponent method to draw the result. This technique was described in Section 8.8. Panel is another example of an inner class. We could have declared Panel as a separate, outer, class. However, in that case, Panel would not have had access to MultiplyApplet's member variables, such as result, unless we declared these public. Note that we still use the AWT Graphics object in Swing. We can use the Multiply.html page from Section 8.10 to run this applet.

8.10.2 Applet Life Cycle Methods

Because applets are run from browsers, they differ from applications in that they do not have a main method. Instead, applets have an init method that is used to perform any applet initialization and is called only once in the lifetime of an applet.

The first method the Web browser invokes on loading the applet is the constructor. In MultiplyApplet, we could have overridden the MultiplyApplet constructor to perform some applet initialization. However, it is not always possible to perform all initialization within an applet constructor. For this reason, the applet class provides the init method, which is invoked after the applet object has been created.

The start method is invoked immediately after the init method. start, as the name suggests, starts the applet execution. start is also invoked if the user revisits the page containing the applet, having left it to visit other Web pages.

The stop method is used to stop the applet's execution, and is invoked when the user quits the browser or leaves the applet's page to visit other Web pages.

The destroy method is invoked after the stop method when the user quits the browser. The applet is unloaded, and any final cleanup actions, such as freeing up memory, are performed by this method.

Note that all these methods belong to the Applet class, and are inherited by the JApplet class, and so apply to both Swing and AWT applets.

8.10.3 Applet Security

Because an applet, resident on a Web server, is invoked by a browser on a client machine, most browsers place security restrictions on what an applet can do on a client machine. For example, applets cannot read, write, delete files, or list directories on the client machine. Applets cannot make network connections other than to the Web server it was loaded from. Applets cannot start new programs. Applets cannot read certain system properties such as the user's home directory or account name. The applet code cannot contain native methods, that is, methods written in a language other than Java.

Note that some browsers relax some of these restrictions when dealing with trusted, or signed, applets. An applet is held in a digitally signed jar (Java Archive) file. The technique of digitally signing a jar file is beyond the scope of this book. The recipient of this signed applet uses encryption techniques to verify the source of the applet. The applet is then "trusted" to perform most of the activities barred to untrusted applets.

chapter **9**

Collections

The Java Collections Framework consists of a number of interfaces and implementations for handling collections and maps. A **collection** groups multiple elements into a single unit. A collection can be implemented as either of the classic data structures, lists or sets. A **list** allows duplicates, and maintains objects in the order in which they are added to the list. On the other hand, a **set** does not allow duplicates and provides either no particular ordering or an ordering based on the objects themselves regardless of the order in which they were added.

A **map** is a grouping of keys and their corresponding values. A map cannot contain duplicate keys, and each key can have at most one associated value. An example of a map is a grouping of employee numbers (key) and the associated employee names (values).

The Collection Framework is a hierarchy of interfaces, as shown in Figure 9.1. This hierarchy is mirrored in the hierarchy of offered implementations, as shown in Figure 9.2. Collections provide examples of polymorphism: some operations are defined on all collections, and as collections get more specialized, operations that make sense only for that type are introduced into the hierarchy. We can write code that will manipulate a Collection type. This code will work regardless of the implementation of that Collection type.

The main top-level interfaces in the Collections Framework are Collection and Map. These interfaces define methods typically for adding elements to, removing elements from, and iterating through collections and maps. Sun does not provide a direct implementation of the Collection interface. Two more interfaces are inherited from the Collection interface: the Set and List interfaces. The SortedSet interface, in turn, inherits from the Set interface. Sun provides classes that implement all these lower-level interfaces. The SortedMap interface inherits from the Map interface; implementations are provided for both the Map and SortedMap interfaces.

9.1 Set Interface

A Set is a collection that cannot contain duplicate elements. This is identical to the mathematical definition of a set. All the methods in the Set interface are inherited from the Collection

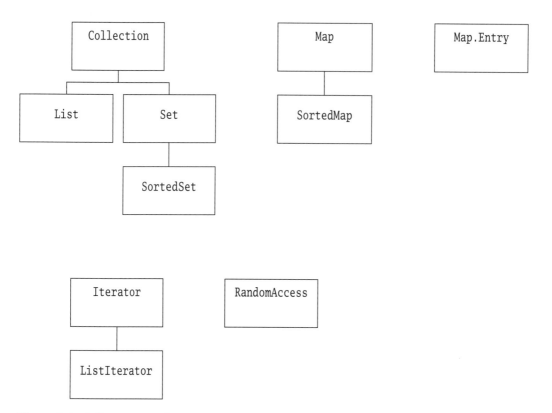

Figure 9.1: Collections interface hierarchy.

interface. Two classes in the java.util package implement the Set interface: HashSet and TreeSet. HashSet is faster but does not guarantee ordering; if ordering is required, TreeSet should be used. TreeSet is a sorted set that we cover in Section 9.1.1.

CollectExample adds an number of elements to a HashSet, then prints the set.

CollectExample

```
1   import java.util.*;
2
3   public class CollectExample {
4
5       public static void main(String[] args) {
6           Collection c = new HashSet();
7           c.add("Smith");
8           c.add("Jones");
9           c.add("Smith");
```

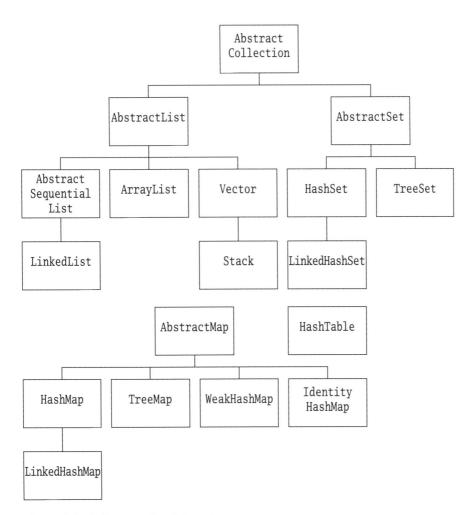

Figure 9.2: Collections class hierarchy.

```
10          c.add("Brown");
11          c.add("Able");
12          Iterator i = c.iterator();
13          while (i.hasNext() ) {
14              System.out.print(i.next() + " ");
15          }
16      }
17  }
```

The output from `CollectExample` is

```
> java CollectExample
Jones Smith Brown Able
```

Note that since duplicates are not allowed in sets, the set contains only one element named "Smith". Note (line 6) that we have defined our HashSet as a Collection type, c. We could have defined the HashSet as a Set type, as follows:

```
Set c = new HashSet();
```

However, as we shall see, using a Collection type makes writing generic code easier. A HashSet has a backing hash table of default initial capacity of 16 buckets (in J2SE 1.4) and load factor of 0.75. This means the hash table is allowed to become three quarters full before it is increased. We can change these default tuning parameters by the constructors HashSet(int capacity) and HashSet(int capacity, float load_factor).

Elements are added to the set using the add method. The Iterator object, which is part of the Collection interface, is used for traversing over collections. The Iterator has three associated methods.

hasNext()	returns true if the iteration has more elements
next()	returns the next element in the iteration
remove()	removes the current element in the iteration from the collection

The program uses the hasNext and next methods to print the entire collection. The following code fragment is used to remove "Brown" from the collection using the Iterator remove method. Note that the Iterator next method returns an Object type.

```
Iterator i = c.iterator();
while (i.hasNext() ) {
    Object o = i.next();
    if (o.equals("Brown") ) {
        i.remove();
    }
}
```

We could remove "Brown" from the collection using the Collection remove method, as follows:

```
c.remove("Brown");
```

The Collection interface has a number of methods for performing bulk operations such as addAll and removeAll. For example, suppose we create a second collection c2, as follows:

```
Collection c2 = new HashSet();
c2.add("Thomas");
c2.add("Able");
```

The statement

```
c.addAll(c2);
```

adds the contents of c2 to c. This is equivalent to a mathematical set union. The resulting contents of c will be "Smith", "Jones", "Brown", "Able", and "Thomas". The statement

```
c.removeAll(c2);
```

removes the contents of c2 from c, or put another way, the result is the set of elements in c that are not in c2. This is equivalent to a mathematical set difference. The resulting contents of c will be "Smith", "Jones", and "Brown". Details of all the Set interface methods and their implementations can be found in the Sun API documentation.

9.1.1 SortedSet Interface

In the previous section, we discussed the HashSet implementation of the Set interface. If we wish to maintain a set in ascending order, we need to use the TreeSet implementation of the SortedSet interface. In CollectExample, we need to replace line 6 with

```
Collection c = new TreeSet();
```

No other changes need to be made. The program output will now be

```
> java CollectExample
Able Brown Jones Smith
```

The order of this SortedSet is a consequence of the String class implementing the Comparable interface. There is only one method in Comparable, namely, compareTo. The compareTo method determines the ordering; in the case of the String implementation of compareTo, this is in lexicographic order. The Java Integer class (the object wrapper for int) and Date class, for example, also implement the Comparable interface. The Integer class compareTo method sorts the set in signed numerical order. The Date class compareTo method sorts the set in chronological order. In Section 9.1.2, we shall see how we might implement our own Comparable interface.

The SortedSet interface inherits all the methods of the Set interface. In addition, SortedSet provides a number of methods, such as first and last, which make sense only for a set that is sorted. There is only one implementation of SortedSet, namely, TreeSet. To use the noninherited methods, we need to replace the statement

```
Collection c = new TreeSet();
```

with

```
SortedSet c = new TreeSet();
```

The statements

```
System.out.println("first: " + c.first());
System.out.println("last: " + c.last());
```

will produce the output

```
first: Able
last: Smith
```

9.1.2 Implementing the Comparable Interface

Suppose we have an Employee class, with attributes employee number, name, and salary. We then create some Employee objects, and then add these to a SortedSet Collection. To keep these in a sorted order, we must implement the Comparable interface compareTo method. This method will define the sort order. The listing shows how we might do this for the Employee class.

Employee

```
1   class Employee implements Comparable {
2       int empNumber;
3       String name;
4       int salary;
5
6       public Employee(int empNumber, String name, int salary) {
7           this.empNumber = empNumber;
8           this.name = name;
9           this.salary = salary;
10      }
11
12      public boolean equals(Object o) {
13          if (o == this) {
14              return true;
15          }
16          if (o == null) {
17              return false;
18          }
19          if (getClass() != o.getClass() ) {
20              return false;
21          }
22          Employee e = (Employee) o;
23          return empNumber == e.empNumber
24                  && name.equals(e.name)
25                  && salary == e.salary;
26      }
27
28      public int hashCode() {
29          int result = 17;
30
31          result = 37 * result + empNumber;
32          result = 37 * result + name.hashCode();
33          result = 37 * result + salary;
34          return result;
35      }
36
37      public int compareTo (Object o) {
```

```
38          Employee e = (Employee) o;
39          return salary - e.salary;
40      }
41  }
```

Employee

In line 1, the Employee class definition indicates that the Comparable interface is being implemented. Lines 6-10 define the Employee constructor. In lines 12-26, we override the equals method, as discussed in Section 5.2.1. In this case, two employee objects are equal if the contents of their empNumber, name, and salary fields are all equal. In lines 28-35, we override the hashCode method, as discussed in Section 5.2.2. If we do not override hashCode, a collection of Employee objects will not behave correctly. In lines 37-40, we define the compareTo method.

The Java Language Specification states the properties that an overridden compareTo method should exhibit. The main requirement is that the expression x.compareTo(y) will return a negative integer, zero, or a positive integer if the object x is less than, equal to, or greater than the object y. In our case, we want to sort according to salary order; since salary is a positive int, the expression salary - e.salary in line 39 satisfies the compareTo requirement.

CreateEmployee creates five employee objects, adds them to a TreeSet collection, and then prints the set.

CreateEmployee

```
1   import java.util.*;
2
3   class CreateEmployee {
4       public static void main(String[] args) {
5           Employee emp1 = new Employee(1, "JONES", 15000);
6           Employee emp2 = new Employee(2, "SIM", 20000);
7           Employee emp3 = new Employee(3, "JONES", 19000);
8           Employee emp4 = new Employee(4, "THORPE", 18000);
9           Employee emp5 = new Employee(3, "JONES", 19000);
10
11          Collection c = new TreeSet();
12          c.add(emp1);
13          c.add(emp2);
14          c.add(emp3);
15          c.add(emp4);
16          c.add(emp5);
17          Iterator i = c.iterator();
18          while (i.hasNext() ) {
19              Employee e = (Employee) i.next();
```

```
20              System.out.println(e.empNumber + " " + e.name
21              + " " + e.salary);
22          }
23      }
24  }
```

CreateEmployee

Note emp1 and emp3 are two different employees with the same surname JONES. Note that emp5 is a duplicate entry for employee number 3. The output, in salary order, is as follows:

```
> java CreateEmployee
1 JONES 15000
4 THORPE 18000
3 JONES 19000
2 SIM 20000
```

Note that, being a set, the collection does not include the duplicate emp5.

Suppose we want to sort by name and salary so that employees with the same name are ordered by salary. The code shows a new version of the Employee class compareTo method.

compareTo

```
1  public int compareTo(Object o) {
2      Employee e = (Employee) o;
3      int cmp = name.compareTo(e.name);
4      return (cmp != 0  ? cmp: salary - e.salary) ;
5  }
```

compareTo

In line 2, we cast the argument o to an Employee type. In line 3, we compare the most significant part of the objects, in this case, name. We use the String.compareTo method for this purpose: this uses a lexicographic ordering as we have seen. cmp will be set to zero if the objects are equal; otherwise, cmp will be nonzero. In line 4, if the value of cmp is nonzero, we return the value of cmp; otherwise, we compare the next significant part of the objects, namely, salary, and return the expression salary - e.salary. If we now run CreateEmployee, the result will be as follows:

```
> java CreateEmployee
1 JONES 15000
3 JONES 19000
2 SIM 20000
4 THORPE 18000
```

9.2 List Interface

A list is an ordered collection that may include duplicate elements. The user has control over positional placing of elements in a list. The List interface, as well as inheriting all the Collection methods, includes additional methods that manipulate the position of elements in a list. Three classes in the java.util package implement the List interface: ArrayList, LinkedList, and Vector. ArrayList, in general, is the fastest implementation; if, however, elements are frequently added to the beginning or end of a list or there are frequent deletions from a list, then the LinkedList implementation should be used. Prior to Java version 1.2, Vector was a separate data structure, since version 1.2 Vector is an implementation of the List interface. The Vector class is similar to an ArrayList; however, Vector is synchronized while ArrayList is unsynchronized. All Collection framework implementations, apart from Vector and Hashtable, are unsynchronized. We discuss synchronization in Section 10.5.

Consider CollectExample from Section 9.1; instead of adding elements to a set, we will add them to a list using the ArrayList implementation. The only change we need to make to the program is to replace line 6 with

```
Collection c = new ArrayList();
```

The program will now output:

```
> java CollectExample
Smith Jones Smith Brown Able
```

Note that since we have a list, the duplicate elements "Smith" are permitted. This example illustrates the polymorphic behavior of Collections. Our Collection interface methods work regardless of whether the implementation is a Set or List.

If we want to use the LinkedList or Vector implementations in the program we only need to change the one statement. Both ArrayList and Vector have a default initial capacity of ten elements. This is automatically incremented when the list becomes full. We can change these default tuning parameters with the constructors ArrayList(int capacity) and Vector(int capacity). There are no tuning parameters for the LinkedList constructor.

There are a number of methods in the List interface such as set, get, and subList that are not inherited from the Collection interface. To use any of these methods, we replace the Collection type in line 6 with a List type, as follows:

```
List c = new ArrayList();
```

The set method is used to replace an element in a specified position in a list with a new element. For example, the statement

```
c.set(3, "BROWN");
```

replaces the fourth element (count from zero) "Brown" with "BROWN".

The get method returns the element at the specified position. For example,

```
Object o = c.get(3);
```

returns the fourth element of c.

The subList(startposition, endposition) method is used to create a sublist from the current list starting at startposition inclusive to endposition **exclusive**. For example, the statement

```
List c1 = c.subList(2, 4);
```

creates a sublist c1 with contents "Smith", "Brown".

The List interface also provides its own iterator, ListIterator, in addition to the Collection interface iterator. ListIterator inherits all the methods of Iterator but in addition provides methods such as previous and hasPrevious for iterating through a list in the reverse direction. previous returns the previous element in the list. hasPrevious returns true if there are more elements in the list when iterating in the reverse direction.

The statement

```
ListIterator l = c.listIterator(5);
```

creates a ListIterator, l, starting at the fourth (last) element in the list c. The argument, 5, is the element that would be retrieved by a call to the next method. The following code fragment iterates backward through our list:

```
while (l.hasPrevious() ) {
    System.out.print(l.previous() + " ");
}
```

producing the result

```
Able Brown Smith Jones Smith
```

Details of all the List interface methods and their implementations can be found in the Sun API documentation.

9.3   Map Interface

A map is a grouping of keys and their corresponding values. A map cannot contain duplicate keys, and each key can have at most one associated value. Recall that a map is a top-level interface, so it does not inherit any of the Collection methods but is provided with its own methods similar in functionality to Collection methods. We will discuss three of the classes in the java.util package that implement the Map interface: HashMap, TreeMap, and Hashtable. HashMap is fastest but does not guarantee ordering; if ordering is required, TreeMap should be used. Prior to Java version 1.2, Hashtable was a separate data structure, since version 1.2, Hashtable is an implementation of the Map interface. The Hashtable class is similar to a HashMap, but a Hashtable is synchronized.

MapExample adds a number of elements to a HashMap, then prints the values of the map.

MapExample

```
1   import java.util.*;
2
```

```
 3  public class MapExample {
 4
 5      public static void main(String[] args) {
 6          Map m = new HashMap();
 7          m.put(new Integer(1), "Smith");
 8          m.put(new Integer(2), "Jones");
 9          m.put(new Integer(3), "Smith");
10          m.put(new Integer(4), "Brown");
11          m.put(new Integer(5), "Able");
12
13          Collection c = m.keySet();
14          Iterator i = c.iterator();
15          while (i.hasNext() ) {
16              System.out.print( m.get(i.next()) + " ");
17          }
18      }
19  }
```

MapExample

The output of the program is

> `java MapExample`
`Able Brown Smith Jones Smith`

Note (line 6) that we have defined our HashMap as a Map type, m. We could have defined the HashMap as a HashMap type, as follows:

`HashMap m = new HashMap();`

However, as with a Collection, a Map type makes the code more generic: the code that follows the preceding statement will work whatever the implementation. To use a Hashtable implementation, we simply change the statement to

`Map m = new Hashtable();`

for the program to work.

In lines 7–11, we use the put(key, value) method to add pairs of keys with associated values to our map. Because the put arguments must be Object types, we use the Integer wrapper to convert integer numbers to objects.

There is no iterator object that iterates directly over a map. We need to use a collection or set view method that converts a map to a collection or set. We then iterate over this collection or set as before. The statement (line 13)

`Collection c = m.keySet();`

uses the collection view method keySet to return a collection, c, of keys contained in the map, m. In lines 15–17, we then iterate over the collection c. In line 16, we use the Iterator.next method to obtain the next key in the collection. We look up the key's value using the Map.get method and print this value. Note that although in this case the map has been ordered by descending key order, the HashMap class does not guarantee ordering. If order has to be guaranteed, we must use the SortedMap interface as described in Section 9.3.1.

Apart from keySet, the other set view methods are values, which returns a collection of values contained in the map, and entrySet, which returns a collection of key value mappings contained in the map. In the preceding MapExample, the entrySet view would be

```
5=Able 4=Brown 3=Smith 2=Jones 1=Smith
```

Details of all the Map interface methods and their implementations can be found in the Sun API documentation.

9.3.1 SortedMap Interface

In the previous section, we discussed the HashMap implementation of the Map interface. If we wish to maintain a map in ascending key order, we need to use the TreeMap implementation of the Map interface. In MapExample, we need to replace line 6 with

```
Map m = new TreeMap();
```

No other changes need to be made. The program output will now be

```
Smith Jones Smith Brown Able
```

The SortedMap interface inherits all the methods of the Map interface. In addition, SortedMap provides a number of methods, such as firstKey and lastKey, which make sense only for a map that is sorted. There is only one implementation of SortedMap, namely, TreeMap. To use the noninherited methods, we need to replace line 6 with

```
SortedMap m = new TreeMap();
```

The statements

```
System.out.println("first key: " + m.firstKey());
System.out.println("last key: " + m.lastKey());
```

will produce the output

```
first key: 1
last key: 5
```

9.4 The Collections Class

The java.util.Collections class provides a number of methods that operate on collections (in most cases, lists). We will describe two such methods, sort and reverse, in this section. The sort method sorts a list into the natural ascending order of its elements. Suppose we have created the following list:

```
List c = new ArrayList();
c.add("Smith");
```

```
c.add("Jones");
c.add("Smith");
c.add("Brown");
c.add("Able");
```

then the statement

```
Collections.sort(c);
```

will sort the List c as follows:

```
Able Brown Jones Smith Smith
```

Like SortedSets, the sort method uses the String class implementation of the Comparable interface compareTo method to sort the Strings in lexicographic order. Similarly, if the collection contains Dates, then the Date class implementation of the Comparable interface compareTo method is used to sort the Dates in chronological order.

The reverse method reverses the order of elements in a list. For example, the statement

```
Collections.reverse(c);
```

will reverse the List c as follows:

```
Able Brown Smith Jones Smith
```

Details of all the Collections class methods can be found in the Sun API documentation.

chapter **10**

Threads

It is possible in Java for an individual program to simultaneously perform more than one task, or **thread**. All the programs discussed in this book so far implicitly use just one thread. Such a program is described as single threaded. Threads cannot exist independently; they always exist within the context of a program. A Java program can have any number of associated threads that are created explicitly; if a program has more than one associated thread, it is said to be multithreaded. Threads are sometimes described as **execution contexts**.

It is possible to delay execution of a thread: this feature of threads is typically used in animation. Multithreading is often used in applets that perform a number of independent tasks, one or more of which performs some lengthy initialization. With multithreading, the applet can perform some tasks while the lengthy tasks continue in the background. Typically, these lengthy tasks include loading images or accessing large volumes of data. A common use of multithreading is in client–server applications where the server may use one thread for each client.

10.1 The Thread Class

Java provides the java.lang.Thread class for explicitly creating and controlling threads. To use threads, first create a subclass of Thread. This subclass must include a run method; the code within the run method performs the thread's task. Each instantiation of this subclass corresponds to a single thread. To start the thread, the controlling program invokes the java.lang.Thread.start method. Invoking start causes the thread's run method to be invoked. This is done right away; we do not wait for another thread to complete the run method. In this way, multithreaded execution is achieved. The thread is implicitly stopped as soon as the run method terminates. One important method in the Thread class is sleep: this causes the thread to cease execution for a specified number of milliseconds.

10.2 Multithreaded Application Example

To illustrate what we have covered so far, we introduce a Java application, PrintNumbersThread, which includes thread code that simply lists the numbers 1 to 10. The application will have two thread instances; the thread will append the thread instance name to the output number so that we can distinguish between the instances. Finally, we will use the sleep method within the thread's run method to cease execution every half-second so that we can interleave the two thread instances' output.

PrintNumbersThread

```
1  public class PrintNumbersThread extends Thread {
2      String name;
3
4      public PrintNumbersThread(String threadName){
5          name = threadName;
6      }
7
8      public void run() {
9          int i;
10
11         for (i=1; i<11; i++) {
12             System.out.println(name + ": " + i);
13             try {
14                 Thread.sleep(500);
15             } catch (InterruptedException e) {}
16         }
17     }
18 }
```

PrintNumbersThread

Line 1 indicates that PrintNumbersThread is a Thread subclass. The PrintNumbersThread class contains a constructor (lines 4-6) that simply assigns the supplied thread's instance name to the variable name. The run method (lines 8-17) contains a for loop that is executed ten times. Within the for loop (line 12), we print the thread instance's name followed by the numbers 1 to 10. In line 14, we use the sleep method to cease the current thread's execution for 500 milliseconds. This will enable any other started threads to resume execution. To use the sleep method, we must enclose the sleep statement within a try catch statement that handles an InterruptedException. Failure to do so will cause the program's compilation to fail.

The RunThreads application invokes PrintNumbersThread.

RunThreads

```
 1  public class RunThreads {
 2
 3      public static void main(String args[]) {
 4          PrintNumbersThread thread1;
 5          PrintNumbersThread thread2;
 6
 7          thread1 = new PrintNumbersThread("Thread1");
 8          thread2 = new PrintNumbersThread("Thread2");
 9          thread1.start();
10          thread2.start();
11      }
12  }
```

RunThreads

In lines 7–8, we create two instances of the thread, thread1 and thread2, by invoking the PrintNumbersThread constructor. In lines 9–10, we use the java.lang.Thread.start method to start the two thread instances.

The output of RunThreads is as follows:

```
> java RunThreads
Thread1: 1
Thread2: 1
Thread1: 2
Thread2: 2
Thread1: 3
Thread2: 3
Thread1: 4
Thread2: 4
Thread1: 5
Thread2: 5
Thread1: 6
Thread2: 6
Thread1: 7
Thread2: 7
Thread1: 8
Thread2: 8
Thread1: 9
Thread2: 9
Thread1: 10
Thread2: 10
```

10.3   Thread Priorities

By default, a thread inherits its priority from the program or thread that created it. It is possible to set a thread's priority using the Thread.setPriority method. A runnable thread with the highest priority is chosen first for execution. The setPriority method takes a value between Thread.MIN_PRIORITY and Thread.MAX_PRIORITY as an argument.

For example, in RunThreads, if we were to add the following statements prior to starting the threads:

```
thread1.setPriority(Thread.MIN_PRIORITY);
thread2.setPriority(Thread.MAX_PRIORITY);
```

the result would be to output the thread2 stream first. The two threads would still be interleaved because the result of using the sleep method on the higher priority thread2 is to allow execution of the lower priority thread1.

Note that the Java thread priority scheduler does not usurp any timeslicing performed on a single-processor computer system using an operating system such as Windows NT. For example, if we were to remove the sleep method (line 14) from the run method of PrintNumbersThread but set the thread priorities as described earlier, we would output all of thread2 followed by all of thread1. On a single-processor timeslicing system, such as Windows NT, the timeslice would be large enough to output the threads in their entirety. However, if our program were modified so that each thread output many thousands of lines, not just ten, then the timeslicing would come into play switching between threads after several thousand iterations of each thread.

10.4   The Runnable Interface

In Section 10.2, we developed a threaded application by extending the Thread class and creating a run method within the extended class. An applet is created by extending the Applet or JApplet class; a class cannot be a subclass of more than one parent class, so we cannot extend the Thread class if we want to create a thread within an applet. To get around this, Java provides the Runnable interface. The interface is specified in the applet class declaration using the implements keyword, for example,

```
public class ThreadedNumbers extends Applet implements Runnable {
```

The Runnable interface consists of just one method, run, which takes no arguments. We create the run method within our applet subclass; the method contains the execution code for the thread similar to the run method for applications described in Section 10.2. We avoid having to subclass Thread by passing an instance of the applet subclass, this, to the newly created Thread object. For example,

```
numbersThread = new Thread(this);
```

The thread is then started as follows:

```
numbersThread.start();
```

10.4.1 Finite Applet Thread Example

Before describing a threaded applet example, OneToTwenty is an applet that paints the numbers 1 to 20 in the applet window. The result is shown in Figure 10.1.

OneToTwenty

```
1   import java.applet.*;
2   import java.awt.Graphics;
3
4   public class OneToTwenty extends Applet {
5
6       public void paint(Graphics g) {
7           int i;
8           int xpos;
9           int ypos;
10          String text;
11
12          xpos = 0;
13          ypos = 50;
14          for (i=1; i<21; i++) {
15              xpos = xpos + 20;
16              text = Integer.toString(i);
17              g.drawString(text, xpos, ypos);
18          }
19      }
20  }
```

OneToTwenty

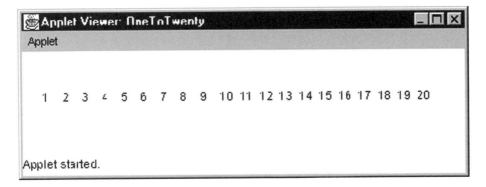

Figure 10.1: Applet Viewer invoking OneToTwenty applet.

The code for the corresponding HTML page, OneToTwenty.html, can be found on the book's Web site. We want to modify the output shown in Figure 10.1 so that each number is painted in turn from left to right at intervals of half a second. This is a simple example of animation, and we would create the code for it by using the Runnable interface described in Section 10.4. This is achieved by ThreadedNumbers.

ThreadedNumbers

```
1   import java.applet.*;
2   import java.awt.Graphics;
3
4   public class ThreadedNumbers extends Applet implements Runnable {
5       Thread numbersThread;
6       int xpos = 0;
7       int ypos = 0;
8       String text = " ";
9
10      public void start() {
11          numbersThread = new Thread(this);
12          numbersThread.start();
13      }
14
15      public void run() {
16          int i;
17
18          xpos = 0;
19          ypos = 50;
20          for (i=1; i<21; i++) {
21              try {
22                  Thread.sleep(500);
23              } catch (InterruptedException e) {}
24              xpos = xpos + 20;
25              text = Integer.toString(i);
26              repaint();
27          }
28      }
29
30      public void paint(Graphics g) {
31          g.drawString(text, xpos, ypos);
32      }
33  }
```

ThreadedNumbers

Line 4 specifies in the applet class declaration that a Runnable interface is being implemented.

The start method (lines 10-13) overrides the applet class start method. In line 11, we pass an instance of the ThreadedNumbers class, this, as an argument to the Thread constructor. In line 12, the thread, numbersThread, is started.

Recall that starting a thread invokes the thread's run method. The run method (lines 15-28) includes a for loop that iterates over the numbers 1 to 20. For each iteration, we delay the thread's execution for half a second, 500 milliseconds, by means of the sleep method (line 22). In lines 24-25, we calculate the string equivalent, text, of the current iteration number and the horizontal position, xpos, of the number.

In line 26, we force the redrawing of the applet window by invoking the repaint method, which in turn, invokes the paint method. The thread is implicitly stopped as soon as the run method terminates.

10.4.2 Infinite Applet Thread Example

In the previous example, the thread stopped as soon as its run method terminated. However, if an applet executes a thread that is terminated only when the user closes or stops the applet, then we need to stop the thread in a different manner. This is best illustrated with an example: the ThreadForEver applet displays integers in turn starting at 1, incrementing the integer by 1, and only terminating when the user stops the applet.

ThreadForEver

```
1   import java.applet.*;
2   import java.awt.Graphics;
3
4   public class ThreadForEver extends Applet
5                               implements Runnable {
6       Thread numbersThread;
7       int i = 1;
8       int xpos = 100;
9       int ypos = 50;
10      String text = " ";
11
12      public void start() {
13          numbersThread = new Thread(this);
14          numbersThread.start();
15      }
16
17      public void run() {
18          while (numbersThread != null) {
19              i++;
20              try {
21                  Thread.sleep(100);
22              } catch (InterruptedException e) {}
23              text = Integer.toString(i);
```

```
24                    repaint();
25          }
26      }
27
28      public void paint(Graphics g) {
29              g.drawString(text, xpos, ypos);
30      }
31
32      public void stop() {
33              numbersThread = null;
34      }
35  }
```

The code for the corresponding HTML page, ThreadForEver.html, can be found on the book's Web site. The applet implements a Runnable interface in the same manner as a finite applet thread. There is also no change to the applet start method. However, instead of a finite for loop in the run method, we specify the following while loop (line 18):

```
while (numbersThread != null) {
```

As long as the thread is not stopped, this condition will be satisfied. The run method delays execution for 100 milliseconds; this is not strictly required but is probably the minimum amount of time required to see individual integers appear on the screen. In lines 23–24, the string equivalents of the integers are displayed in the same position in the applet window using the repaint and paint methods as before.

The stop method overrides the applet class stop method. This method is invoked when the user either stops or quits the applet using Applet Viewer or closes the window with a browser. The stop method consists of just one statement (line 33) setting the numbersThread object to null, thus causing the while loop in the run method to terminate.

10.5 Synchronizing Threads

A program may access the same object from separate concurrent threads. To ensure that only one thread at a time can access an object, we use the **synchronized** keyword. We can synchronize a method or block of code. When a thread executes a synchronized method or block of code, it places a lock on the associated object. This prevents any other thread from executing any synchronized method that accesses that object.

For example, the SynchronizedSumming class contains two synchronized methods, add and subtract.

SynchronizedSumming

```
1  public class SynchronizedSumming{
2      int result;
3
4      synchronized void add(int arg1) {
5          result = result + arg1;
6      }
7
8      synchronized void subtract(int arg1) {
9          result = result - arg1;
10     }
11 }
```

SynchronizedSumming

Any thread concurrently executing either of these methods is accessing the same shared SynchronizedSumming object. In particular, the SynchronizedSumming result variable is shared. So we do not want one thread to be executing the add method while another is concurrently executing the subtract method.

As soon as the first thread executes the add method, say, because it is synchronized, a lock is placed on the SynchronizedSumming object. This prevents another thread from executing any synchronized method that accesses the SynchronizedSumming object. In particular, a second thread cannot execute the subtract method. As soon as the first thread completes execution of the add method, the lock on the object is released.

Rather than place a lock on an object for the duration of an entire method, we may be able to isolate critical lines of code that access an object. For example, the add method may perform some time-consuming processing that does not affect the SynchronizedSumming object until the last statement. We can create a synchronized block around this statement as follows:

```
void add(int arg1) {
    ...
    time consuming processing statements
    ...
    synchronized (this) {
        result = result + arg1;
    }
}
```

The this keyword ensures the current object, SynchronizedSumming, is locked. If the synchronized block accesses another object, object_name, say, that we want to lock, we would use the statement

```
synchronized (object_name) {
```

10.6   Thread States

In the previous sections, we talked about starting a thread, delaying execution of a thread by means of the sleep method, and stopping a thread. In this section, we describe the various thread states more precisely. A thread can be in one of the following states:

- **New thread.** A thread is in this state after it has been created using the Thread constructor but before the start method has been invoked. A new thread will have no system resources allocated for it.

- **Runnable.** A thread becomes runnable when the start method is invoked. This does not mean that a thread is actually running; in a single-processor computer system, another thread may be running at a given moment.

- **Not runnable.** A thread cannot run. A thread becomes not runnable when the Thread class sleep or wait method has been invoked.

- **Dead.** A thread dies when it stops. This occurs automatically when the thread's run method terminates.

Finally, the Thread class includes a method isAlive to test if a thread is **alive**. A thread is alive if it has been started and has not yet died. If a thread is alive, it is either runnable or not runnable. One cannot distinguish one state from the other. If a thread is not alive, it is either a new thread or dead. Again, it is not possible to distinguish between these states.

Operator Precedence

The following table lists Java's operators and associativity characteristics in order of precedence. Operators at the top of the table have greater precedence than those lower down.

Operator Level	Associativity
++ --	right to left
! ~ cast	right to left
* / %	left to right
+ -	left to right
<< >> >>>	left to right
< > <= >= instanceof	left to right
== !=	left to right
&	left to right
^	left to right
|	left to right
&&	left to right
||	left to right
?:	right to left
= *= /= %= += -= <<= >>= >>>= &= ^= |=	right to left

appendix **B**

Swing Events

The following table lists the event listeners, the methods that are used in the interface to respond to the events and the Swing components that generate the corresponding events.

Listener Interface	Associated Methods	Invoked by Component
ActionListener	actionPerformed	Button, Check Box, Combo Box, Menu Item, Radio Button, Text Field, File Chooser, Password Field, Toggle Button
CaretListener	caretUpdate	Editor Pane, Password Field, Text Area, Text Field, Text Pane
ComponentListener	componentHidden componentMoved componentResized componentShown	All components and containers
ContainerListener	componentAdded componentRemoved	All containers
ChangeListener	stateChanged	Button, Check Box, Color Chooser, Menu Item, Progress Bar, Radio Button, Slider, Tabbed Pane, Toggle Button, Scroll Pane
DocumentListener	changedUpdate insertUpdate removeUpdate	Editor Pane, Password Field, Text Area, Text Field, Text Pane
UndoableEditListener	undoableEditHappened	Editor Pane, Password Field, Text Area, Text Field, Text Pane
FocusListener	focusGained focusLost	All components and containers

Listener Interface	Associated Methods	Invoked by Component
ItemListener	itemStateChanged	Button, Check Box, Combo Box, Menu Item, Radio Button, Toggle Button
KeyListener	keyPressed keyReleased keyTyped	All components and containers
ListSelectionListener	valueChanged	List, Table
MouseListener	mouseClicked mouseEntered mouseExited mousePressed mouseReleased	All components and containers
MouseMotionListener	mouseDragged mouseMoved	All components and containers
WindowListener	windowActivated windowClosed windowClosing windowDeactivated windowDeiconified windowIconified windowOpened	Dialog, Frame
HyperLinkListener	hyperlinkUpdate	Editor Pane, Text Pane
MenuListener	menuCanceled menuDeselected menuSelected	Menu
MenuKeyListener	menuKeyPressed menuKeyReleased menuKeyTyped	Menu Item
MenuDragMouseListener	menuDragMouseDragged menuDragMouseEntered menuDragMouseExited menuDragMouseReleased	Menu Item
PopupMenuListener	popupMenuCanceled popupMenuWillBecomeInvisible popupMenuWillBecomeVisible	Popup Menu
TableColumnModelListener	columnAdded columnMarginChanged columnMoved columnRemoved columnSelectionChanged	Table
CellEditorListener	editingCanceled editingStopped	Table
TableModelListener	tableChanged	Table

Listener Interface	Associated Methods	Invoked by Component
InternalFrameListener	internalFrameActivated internalFrameClosed internalFrameClosing internalFrameDeactivated internalFrameDeiconified internalFrameIconified internalFrameOpened	Internal Frame
ListDataListener	contentsChanged intervalAdded intervalRemoved	List
TreeExpansionListener	treeCollapsed treeExpanded	Tree
TreeWillExpandListener	treeWillCollapse treeWillExpand	Tree
TreeModelListener	treeNodesChanged treeNodesInserted treeNodesRemoved treeStructureChanged	Tree
TreeSelectionListener	valueChanged	Tree

Index